RPG MAKER II™

PRIMA'S OFFICIAL STRATEGY GUIDE

DAMIEN WAPLES

MICHAEL LITTLEFIELD

Prima Games
A Division of Random House, Inc.
3000 Lava Ridge Court
Roseville, CA 95661
1-800-733-3000
www.primagames.com

Product Manager: Jill Hinckley

Project Editor: Teli Hernandez

Important:

Prima Games has made every effort to determine that the information contained in this book is accurate. However, the publisher makes no warranty, either expressed or implied, as to the accuracy, effectiveness, or completeness of the material in this book; nor does the publisher assume liability for damages, either incidental or consequential, that may result from using the information in this book. The publisher cannot provide information regarding game play, hints and strategies, or problems with hardware or software. Questions should be directed to the support numbers provided by the game and device manufacturers in their documentation. Some game tricks require precise timing and may require repeated attempts before the desired result is achieved.

ISBN: 0-7615-4356-2

Library of Congress Catalog Card Number: 2003109751

Printed in the United States of America

03 04 05 06 LL 10 9 8 7 6 5 4 3 2 1

CONTENTS

INTRODUCTION

Where do we start? That question is worth asking when undertaking any complex project, and creating the guide for *RPG Maker 2* started with that same query. We'll be honest with you: We didn't know what to expect when we started playing this game. We would have hesitated to call it a game at all. It seemed more like a toolset with which to build a game.

When we loaded the "game" up and started playing around with it, we had no idea how to proceed. We didn't have a manual or an in-game tutorial to guide us through the basics of creating anything, let alone a full-fledged, original role-playing game. We were lost, but in an author's life, that's nothing new!

So we did what we always do. We played anyway. We played around with all the little pieces, even though we had no idea how they should fit together or even if they were supposed to fit together.

But something happened as we struggled to figure out the nuances. We began to see what was possible with the tools we were given. And the more clearly we saw the possibilities, the more we wanted to figure out how to get there. In essence, the more we played with it, the more it became a game.

It is easy to get mired in the details. It takes patience and time to see the bigger picture—to see how much you can do with what has been provided. Truly, your imagination is the limit. You get out of the game what you put in. You can choose to alter pre-existing data and insert an original story, or you can create the entire world, from the ground up.

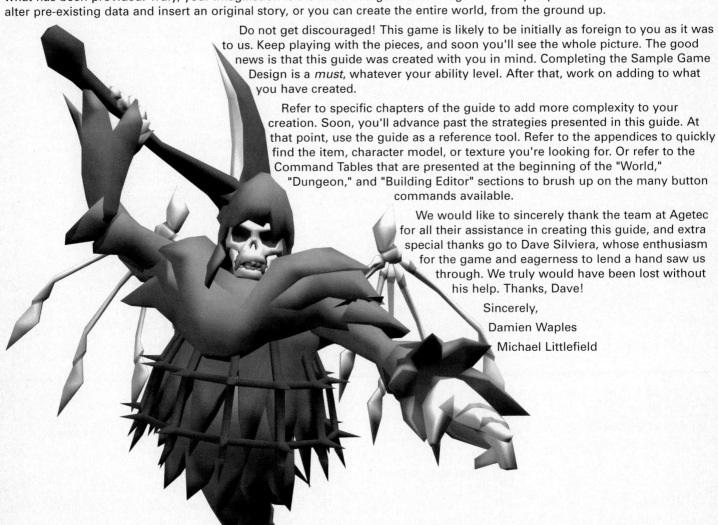

Do not get discouraged! This game is likely to be initially as foreign to you as it was to us. Keep playing with the pieces, and soon you'll see the whole picture. The good news is that this guide was created with you in mind. Completing the Sample Game Design is a *must*, whatever your ability level. After that, work on adding to what you have created.

Refer to specific chapters of the guide to add more complexity to your creation. Soon, you'll advance past the strategies presented in this guide. At that point, use the guide as a reference tool. Refer to the appendices to quickly find the item, character model, or texture you're looking for. Or refer to the Command Tables that are presented at the beginning of the "World," "Dungeon," and "Building Editor" sections to brush up on the many button commands available.

We would like to sincerely thank the team at Agetec for all their assistance in creating this guide, and extra special thanks go to Dave Silviera, whose enthusiasm for the game and eagerness to lend a hand saw us through. We truly would have been lost without his help. Thanks, Dave!

Sincerely,

Damien Waples

Michael Littlefield

SAMPLE GAME DESIGN

Rome wasn't built in a day, but a small adventure can be. The following section takes you through the process of creating a simple adventure. We leave complex descriptions of each step to the more detailed sections that follow. Think of this as a basic tutorial to help you become familiar with the various editors, model databases, and organizational tools that can be used in *RPG Maker 2*.

Don't get discouraged if you initially find yourself confused or can't wrap your mind around the multiple steps required to create even the smallest piece of the puzzle. It all becomes clear as you spend time playing with it.

GETTING STARTED

"The longest journey begins with a single step." Cheap fortune cookie sentiment? Maybe. Accurate? Absolutely! Select "Edit Game" from *RPG Maker 2*'s main menu to begin building your own adventure.

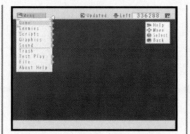

The blue screen that appears with the single tab labeled "Menu" probably isn't what you expected. But contained within the nine menus are all the tools you need to fashion as complex a world as you desire.

SELECTING THE DIFFICULTY LEVEL

Press ✕ to access the menus and select "File" with another press of ✕. Select "New," then "Beg" and you're greeted with a welcome screen. Exit the screen and select "Menu" once again. All the menus are now available.

Select "File," then "Preferences" to open the Preferences menu. Tap ✕ on "User" and again on "Level," then switch the difficulty to "Hard." This may seem redundant, but if you had just selected "Hard" from the outset, no pre-existing data would have been loaded, and you would begin building from scratch. Tap ● three times to exit the "Preferences" menu and select "Update Data and Exit" to update your settings.

Read through the welcome screen to learn that selecting "Beginner" mode limits you to editing pre-existing data only.

SAVING YOUR GAME

You are often prompted to either "Update Data and Exit" or to "Exit Without Updating." Selecting the former keeps your updated settings until you turn off your PlayStation 2, but it does not save your changes to the memory card. To save changes to the memory card, select "File" from the main menu, then select "Save."

Selecting "Exit Without Updating" discards any changes you just made. Select this option when you enter a menu by mistake, or you are not happy with your changes.

To name your saved game file, select "Game" from the main menu, then select "Game Settings." Tap ✕ to select the "Basic" tab, then again to enter the "Game Name" field. Rename the game to "Blamo's Quest," then tap ● to exit the Text Input screen. Select "Update Data and Exit" and you're returned to the Game Settings page. Now select the "Designer" field, and change "Agetec" to your name. Exit, but remember to update your changes.

Always choose the option to update your data, unless you are unhappy with your changes.

CONCEPTUALIZING

What kind of story should we make? In the interest of keeping it simple, let's start out with two townspeople named Blamo and Hooligan who, in their thirst for adventure, undertake a dangerous quest given to them by a distressed Princess. A thief has stolen her ring and taken refuge in a small dungeon. The pair must venture to the dungeon, battle the thief, and reclaim the stolen ring.

Afterward, they can return triumphantly to town, and claim the Princess' gratitude. It's a bit trite, but it includes all the basic elements of a good role-playing game. Now that we have an idea of what we want to make, we can begin the creation process.

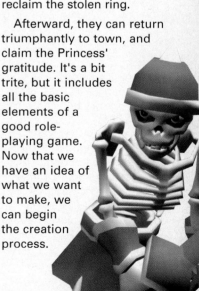

LAYING THE FOUNDATION

RPG Maker 2 allows you to start creating any aspect of the adventure in whatever order you like. For the purposes of this walkthrough, we teach you how to build your adventure from the ground up. Building in a linear fashion makes more sense to the novice.

When you become adept at using all the tools, you may find it is easier to do things out of order. We'll talk more about that in later sections.

CREATING A TOWN FROM PRE-EXISTING DATA

A townsperson turned adventurer needs a town from which to start adventuring, right? Instead of creating one from scratch, we can load a pre-existing model and go from there.

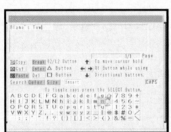

This is the Map database. You can highlight a map to copy or to edit.

Select "Graphics" from the main menu, then highlight and select "Map Editor." The Map database pops up and we can select a map to work with. Move the directional pad up until the cell contents of the database are highlighted. Tap X and move up to File 1, "Preset Town." Tap X once again and select "Copy" from the menu. Press ● and move the directional pad down to highlight "Paste

Copied Data." Select "Paste Copied Data" and the Map Editor screen appears. Select the "Basic" tab, then the "Name" field. Delete "Preset Town" and rename it "Blamo's Town." Tap ● to exit the Text Input screen and return to the Map Editor. Make sure you select the "Update Data and Exit" option.

Tap ● twice to exit the editor making sure to update your changes. "Blamo's Town" now appears in the Map database. Exit the Map Editor and return to the main menu.

This is the Text Input screen. Use a USB keyboard or the graphical interface to input text.

REGISTERING THE MAP

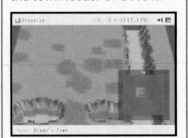

This is the World Organization database. It lists both the pre-existing maps and the maps that you have created and registered.

We need to register the map we just created within "World Organization." You can find it under "Graphics." The World Organization database consists of four files numbered from zero to three. We are going to create a fifth. Select "Create New Data" and

a generic world set page pops up. Select the "Basic" tab and change the name to "Blamo's Town." Exit the Input page and return to the World Organization page.

Now move the directional pad down until "-None-" is highlighted beneath the checked "Map Database" field within the "Data" box. Select "-None-" with a press of X, then tap up on the directional pad until you highlight "Blamo's Town." Select it and you're automatically returned to the World Organization screen.

This is one of the most important screens to become familiar with. Everything that associated with Blamo's Town is selected and linked to it here.

Now that "Preset Town" has been loaded and renamed, let's look at what we have to work with. Tap ● to highlight "Basic," then move over to the "View" button. Select "View" and the town loads. Or does it?

Only the landscape is selected when you choose a map from the Map database or Dungeon database. You must apply an Object Set to see what has been built on the land.

What's the deal? You see grass and water, but no town. Press SELECT to return to the World Organization Editor. Select the "Basic" tab again, then move down to the "Objects" field. Select "-None-" and choose "0001:Preset Town" from the popup menu. Now select "View" again and let's see what appears.

Think of Blamo's Town as it exists in the World Organization database as an empty folder. The files that fill that folder are the Sets. We just called up an Object Set and later we will select an Event Set. When all the Sets are in the file (there are five), the file is complete.

There's the town, complete with several buildings, some trees, gardens, and even a pair of brick pillars at the entrance. Selecting a map (or dungeon) within the Data box only selects the map or dungeon. It does not include anything placed or built upon the land (or within a dungeon). To view objects, which include buildings and items, we needed to select an Object Set within the "Objects" Field. Now that we have, both the map "Preset Town," and the Object Set "Preset Town" appear. Tap SELECT to return to the World Organization Editor.

NOTE

Just as we created Blamo's Town from a pre-existing map called "Preset Town," we also used pre-existing data for our Object Set (it, too, is called "Preset Town"). Had we chosen instead to create our own Object Set, we could have given it a name and then selected it in the "Objects" field rather than "Preset Town." But we're getting ahead of ourselves; we'll talk more about that later.

Tap ● a few times, then "Update Data and Exit." You notice that "Blamo's Town" is now listed in the World Organization database.

HERE THERE BE MONSTERS...

So, we have our town. Now we need to add a dungeon for our intrepid adventurers to explore, and then register it in the World Organization database.

This is the Dungeon database within the Dungeon Editor menu. All created dungeons are listed here.

Exit to the main menu and select "Dungeon Editor" from the Graphics menu. The Dungeon database pops up. We don't want to create a new dungeon from scratch right now, and we also don't want to alter any of the pre-existing maps. So, as we did within the Map Editor, tap the directional pad up until the database spreadsheet is highlighted. Select it and move the cursor over "File 15:Dungeon." Tap ✕ and select "Copy" from the popup menu. Tap ● and select the "Paste Copied Data" button. Select the "Basic" tab, then change the name "Dungeon" to "Blamo's Dungeon." Exit the Dungeon Editor, remembering to update your changes. "Blamo's Dungeon" is now listed within the Dungeon database.

The Dungeon Editor allows you to alter an existing dungeon, copy an existing dungeon, or create a dungeon from scratch. For now, we are simply copying a dungeon and renaming it.

Now we have to register the dungeon within World Organization. Select "Graphics" from the main menu, then "World Organization." Select "Create New Data," select the "Basic" tab and change the generic World Set name to "Blamo's Dungeon." Next, move the directional pad down until "Dungeon Database" is highlighted. Check the bubble, then change "-None-"

to "Blamo's Dungeon." Update your data and exit the World Organization menu.

In addition to the folder called Blamo's Town, we now have an empty file folder called Blamo's Dungeon. Any Set we wish to link with this dungeon is called up from this page.

CREATING THE PARTY

We've created the foundation for our world; now we need to create the adventurers. Our story involves two friends, so that's where we start (we cover the creation of the Princess in a bit).

There are a few steps in creating your party of adventurers. You must select the models for your characters, register them in the Party Member database, then select the ones with which you wish to begin the game.

SELECTING CHARACTER MODELS

You have more than 100 character models to choose from in the Character Models database. All can be customized in a variety of ways.

The first choice in the Graphics menu is "Character Models." Select it to enter the Character Models database. Select "Create New Data" to begin creating the first character in your party. First, highlight and select the "Name" field to edit the name of your character. Name him Blamo, then update your data and exit to return to the Character Editor.

Next, highlight the "Model" field and press ✕. You see nine models from which to choose your character's appearance. Tap right on the directional pad five times to highlight the slider. Tap down on the directional pad once to highlight the slider bar. Now, press and hold ✕ while moving the directional pad down to browse through all 115 models that are available. To move quickly back to the beginning of the model database, tap ✕ while the slider arrow is highlighted. "Model 17:Pirate Captain" suits Blamo just fine, so we'll choose that model for him. You automatically return to the Character Editor after you make your selection.

TIP

Press R1 to move the slider down one row; press L1 to move the slider up one row. If you use L2 and R2, you scroll one page.

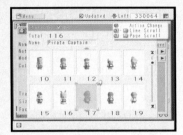

Selecting the "Model" field brings up thumbnails of all the model choices.

CUSTOMIZING YOUR MODEL

We get into the more advanced features of this editor later in the guide, but feel free to play around with the "Color" field now. It works like this: Highlight one of the 16 boxes in the 4x4 color display grid and part of the character's graphic model will blink. Tap **X** on the box to change the color of the blinking portion.

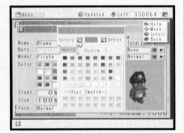

This is the Color Editor. Here you can customize the outward appearance of your model.

For example, Captain Blamo would look much more commanding in a red hat. Plus, it matches his cape. In the interest of vanity and good taste, let's change that for him. Move your cursor through the grid until the Captain's hat is blinking. The hat selection is on the second row, third column from the left. Tap **X** and the Color Editor pops up. Highlight the "Swatch" tab and tap **X**. Highlight the color you like and tap **X**.

Notice the "Before" and "After" fields beneath the "Color Edit" banner. This gives you a graphic comparison of the previous color and the color you have just chosen. When you are happy with your choice, tap ● twice to exit the Color Editor screen. Remember to update your changes. When you are done editing your character's appearance, tap ● to exit the Character Editor, and return to the Character Model database. Blamo should now appear as File #116.

Princesses love a man in uniform!

We need to create one more character in the same way. Select "Create New Data" and follow the same steps to create your second party member. Our second character is Hooligan, Captain Blamo's faithful and whacky sidekick. We've chosen Model 83 for Hooligan, because it looks funny. Hooligan appears as File #117 in the Character Model database after you've exited the Character Editor.

REGISTERING YOUR CHARACTERS AS PARTY MEMBERS

You can choose from among 20 pre-existing party members to either alter or use to fill a party created from scratch.

Now that Blamo and Hooligan appear in the Character Model database with their own color customizations, we need them to appear in the Party Member database. Select "Game" from the main menu, then select "Party Members." Select "Create New Data" and the Party Member Editor pops up. Select the "Name" field and type in your first character's name. This may seem redundant, but remember that you only named a customized model before, not an actual member.

We officially promote Blamo to Captain Blamo and name him appropriately. After exiting the Text Input screen, highlight the "Model" field. Highlight "-None-" and select it with a tap of the **X** button. The Party Member database pops up and "-None-" is highlighted. Tap up on the directional pad twice to highlight the first model you created. We had named our model "Blamo" so that name appears as number 0116. Select that model and you are automatically returned

to the Party Member Editor where the model of "Blamo" now appears.

Creating a new member is as easy as changing the name and selecting a pre-existing model.

EQUIPPING YOUR PARTY

Now we need to equip our adventurer for battle. Select the "Custom" tab, then select "Items." Change the "1" field from "-None-" to item "0017:Mace." Exit the "Items" tab and move down one tab until "Equip" is highlighted. Select it and change the "Weapon" field to: "01:Mace." Captain Blamo now starts the game with a mace automatically equipped.

Exit all the way out to the Party Member database and you notice "Captain Blamo" now appears as number 20 in the Party Member database.

The "Custom" tab allows you to alter everything from starting statistics to magic resistances.

Select "Create New Data" once again and repeat the process to add Hooligan as a party member, and to equip him for battle.

Hooligan appears as Member number 21 in the Party Member database.

SELECTING YOUR PARTY AND SPECIFYING A STARTING LOCATION

The General Settings menu allows you to specify which members start the adventure together, and where exactly they start.

Select "Game" from the main menu, then select "General Settings." The Party Member Selection screen appears, complete with a preset, four-member party. Select the "Basic" tab and "Virk" will be highlighted. Tap ✕, and the Party Member database pops up. Select "Captain Blamo" and a thumbnail image of him appears in the first position.

Next, select "Bryra" and replace her with "Hooligan." Finally, select "Zul" and "Harmony" and replace them with "-None-." Your party now consists of Captain Blamo and Hooligan. Now you must specify at what location they begin the game.

Select a map to be the starting point for the party.

Highlight the field "Preset Town," to the right of the first party member's picture. Tap ✕ and the Map database pops up. We want the party to begin in our created town, so select "Blamo's Town" from the menu. Next, tap the directional pad right one time to highlight the small map placement icon. This loads Blamo's Town.

The location of the yellow diamond indicates the party's initial placement. We want them to start in the middle of town, so move the cursor to about 112,112. You can find the coordinates listed at the top of the screen after "(X, Y, Z)=." The "x" represents east/west location, "y" represents north/south location, and "z" represents altitude. You must find the correct altitude for your members to start at otherwise they might appear under or above the ground. Once you find 112, 112, press and hold [L1] until the yellow diamond stops moving (this automatically determines the correct height for your characters). After you have adjusted the altitude, tap ✕ and the black, semi-transparent box is updated with the party's starting location.

Move the yellow cursor to this position and tap ✕ to set the starting point for the party.

NOTE

The semi-transparent box that takes up the northwest portion of screen shows the party's current starting position. It is not updated until you move the yellow cursor to a new location and tap ✕ to confirm a new starting point. If you simply move the cursor to the new location without tapping ✕, your party still begins at the previous location.

Hit [SELECT] to return to the General Settings menu. Exit General Settings and update data.

OBJECT PLACEMENT

All characters, buildings, and items that cannot be directly interacted with are called objects. The rest are called events. A box that cannot be examined, opened, or talked to is an object. But if a box can be examined, opened, or talked to (you've never heard of a talking box?), it becomes an event. You can place objects on a map; events must be created from scripts, then placed on the map.

This is the Object Placement database. It doesn't list individual objects such as boxes or carpets. Rather, it lists the name of the Object Set (think empty folder) which contains every object placed within it (think files).

Let's place an object so you get the hang of it. To do so, enter the "Object Placement" within the "Graphics" menu. Select "File 1:Preset Town" from the Object Placement database and choose "Copy" from the menu. Move the cursor down and select the "Paste Copied Data" button. Because we want the object to appear within the confines of Blamo's Town, we should name the Object Set appropriately. Highlight the "Name" field, select it and change the name to "BT Objects." This makes your Object Set easily recognizable as the Object Set for Blamo's Town.

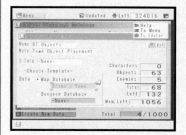

The Object Set we named "BT Objects" comprises all objects we place in Blamo's Town, including the "Stairs Down."

Now, make sure "Blamo's Town" is called out under the "Data:Map Database" field. Next, select "Edit" and Blamo's Town loads. Move the cursor west and outside the town limits to about 90,125. Tap ✕ and a blinking, blue-clad character appears. Tap ■ to change the character model to a blinking barrel. You are now in Object Select mode. Tap right on the directional pad 30 times until item number 31—"Stairs Down"— appears. Tap ✕ and you have placed the "Stairs Down" item on the map. This is the entrance to Blamo's Dungeon. Tap SELECT to exit Blamo's Town, then exit the Object Placement database, remembering to update your data.

While in the Object Placement Editor, tap ■ to cycle the placement set from characters, to objects, to buildings.

NOTE

Browse the object, character, and building appendices in the back of this guide to view the pre-set data available for placement.

REGISTERING YOUR OBJECT SET

To see how the pieces fit together, exit Object Placement Editor, remembering to update your data, and return to the World Organization database within the Graphics menu.

Now, highlight and select "Blamo's Town" in the World Organization database. Select "Edit," then tap ✕ and move the cursor down to the "Objects" field. Make sure the "BT Objects" Object

Set appears in the "Objects" field. Select "View," and after Blamo's Town loads, you'll notice the stairs sitting right where you placed them.

Once your Object Set is registered in the World Organization database, any future objects you place in the Object Placement Editor are automatically updated within the World Organization database.

SCRIPTS AND EVENTS

Now we need to set up a few events. We need the Princess to give our heroes the quest, we need to set up a warp point from the stairs we just placed to the dungeon, and we need to set up a battle between the party and the thief. Finally, we need to have the Princess thank the party for their good deed.

This is the Scripts menu. Everything you need to create scripts and events is found here.

CREATING A DIALOGUE SCRIPT

About 400 pre-existing scripts are available within the Script database to choose or alter.

Enter the "Scripts" menu, then the "Scripts" sub-menu. Select "Create New Data," then change the name "Script 0398" to "Greetings." Exit the Text Input screen and tap down on the directional pad twice to highlight the large white box that takes up the majority of the screen. Tap ✕ and a large menu appears. Move down to "Input Creation" and select it. Select "Multiple Choice" and an input screen appears. Tap the directional pad down once to highlight the "Choices" field. Change the number of choices to "2."

Now move down to highlight the "1" field. Enter the field and type "Yes." Exit and update, then enter the "2" field. Type "No" and exit. Tap ● to exit, update data, and you have five lines of script.

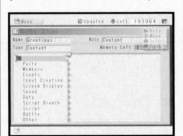

Selecting the large white portion of the screen causes this large menu to pop up.

These five lines are automatically created for you once you specify the parameters of your script.

Tap the directional pad up until the green line is at the top of the script box, above line "000." Tap ✕ and select "Screen Display," "Text," then "Message." Tap ✕ once more and the Text Input screen appears. Type the following: "Hello, Blamo. Will you help me? A thief stole my ring!!" Exit back to the Script Editor, updating your data as prompted.

You've now added the Princess's opening line of dialogue.

Now, move the green line until it rests above "003 Script: Condition End." Tap ✕ and select "Screen Display," "Text," then "Message." Tap ✕ once more and the Text Input screen appears. We are now typing the message that appears when you answer "Yes" to her request. Type: "Oh, thank you, Blamo. The thief left town and headed west. Please get my ring back!" Exit back to the Script Editor page, and update your data when prompted.

What you just entered is the Princess's response if you accept her quest by selecting "Yes."

Once again, move the green line until it rests above "006 Script:Condition End." Tap ✗ and select "Screen Display," "Text," then "Message." Tap ✗ once more and the Text Input screen appears. We are now typing the message that appears when you answer "No" to her request. Type: "How rude. I suppose you expect me to retrieve the ring myself then? Please return when you have reconsidered!" Exit back to the Script Editor page and update your data when prompted.

You are now finished creating the dialogue script for your conversation with the Princess. Now we need to attach the script to a character and place her in the town.

This is the completed dialogue script, including a "No" response. But you wouldn't say no to a Princess, would you?

CREATING A DIALOGUE EVENT FROM YOUR SCRIPT

The Event database contains almost 400 events, composed of countless numbers of scripts.

From the main menu, select "Scripts" then "Events." Select "Create New Data" and change the generic event name to "Greetings." Move the cursor down to the "Model" field and select "0029: Princess." After all, who better to do battle for than a Princess? Now, move down to the "Start" field and select "Talk." This controls how the event is triggered. In this case, the dialogue begins when the Princess is spoken to. Finally, select the "Apply" field and move the cursor to "0398:Greetings." You may want to use R2 and L2 to scroll through the scripts. Select "Greetings" and you have successfully tied your script to a model and created an event!

The Event Editor allows you to control exactly how your script is triggered and applied.

PLACING THE EVENT

The location of the yellow diamond indicates the party's initial placement. We want them to start in the middle of town, so move the cursor to about 112,112. You can find the coordinates listed at the top of the screen after "(X, Y, Z)=." The "x" represents east/west location, "y" represents north/south location, and "z" represents altitude. You must find the correct altitude for your members to start at otherwise they might appear under or above the ground. Once you find 112, 112, press and hold L2 until the yellow diamond stops moving (this automatically determines the correct height for your characters). After you have adjusted the altitude, tap ✗ and the black, semi-transparent box is updated with the party's starting location.

Just as we created a single Object Set for Blamo's Town, we will now create a single Event Set for Blamo's Town.

Select "Create New Data" and change the generic Event Set name to "BT Events." Then, move down to the "Data" box and select "Blamo's Town" in the "Map Database" field. Next, move down to the "Object Set" field and select "BT Objects." We can now place the "Greetings" event on the map of Blamo's Town. Select the "Edit" button and

move the cursor to about 108,112. These coordinates are just west of the starting point we set for our party.

Tap ✗ and a blinking boat appears. Tap left on the directional pad and the "Greetings" event appears as the model of the Princess. Tap ✗ and viola! You have placed your first event. Tap SELECT to exit Blamo's Town, then exit the Event Placement Editor.

All the events you place here become part of the Event Set we titled "BT Events."

Now, we must register our newly created Event Set in the World Organization database so it appears when we test our game.

NOTE

Select "Test Play," then "Start" from the main menu at any time to see how the game is progressing.

REGISTERING THE BLAMO'S TOWN EVENT SET

Select "Blamo's Town" from the World Organization database and "Edit" to bring up the World Organization page for Blamo's Town. Select the "Basic" tab and move the cursor down to the "Events" field. Select "BT Events" from the popup menu. From now on, all the events you place in "Event Placement:BT Events" appear within Blamo's Town. Exit the World Organization Editor.

At this point we have registered both an Object Set and an Event Set for Blamo's Town. For the purposes of this tutorial, the "Blamo's Town" file folder is now complete.

CREATING A WARP SCRIPT

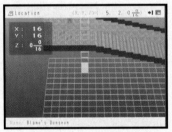

To create a way to warp from one area to another, choose the desired options, then specify a destination.

Now we need to set two warp points so our party can move from Blamo's Town to Blamo's Dungeon, and vice versa. Select "Scripts" from the main menu, then "Scripts" from the sub-menu. Select "Create New Data" and change the generic script name to: "Warp:BT to BD." This designates a one-way warp from Blamo's Town to Blamo's Dungeon. Highlight the large white text box and tap ✕. From the menu, select "Party," then "Teleport," then "Warp."

Now select the warp destination. The "Location" field should be highlighted. Select "-None-" and then select "Blamo's Dungeon" from the popup menu. You notice the X,Y,Z locations have changed to 16,16,0. These are generic coordinates that mark the center of the mapping grid. We want to select our own entry point into the dungeon, so highlight and select the colored placement icon to the right of the "Location" field. Blamo's Dungeon loads and you see that the center of the map grid does not even fall within the walls of the dungeon. Press and hold R1 while rotating the left analog stick counterclockwise to zoom the camera out a bit. Now, move the cursor to 5,2,0.

Placing the pointer selects the destination of the warp. Be careful, though—the yellow portion is where the party will enter.

TIP

If you hold R1 while moving the directional pad, you can rotate the camera to get a better view of the cursor placement.

Notice that the white wire-frame column extends through the platform above the dungeon's stairs, but the

yellow box that dictates where our party appears in the dungeon is well below the platform. To raise the elevation of the yellow box, tap L1 six times. This places the yellow box at 5,2,6, which is right on top of the platform. Tap ✕ to select those coordinates and the black box updates and reflects the party's entry point. Exit back to the Script database page, updating your data as you proceed.

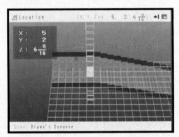

The party now warps onto the platform, rather than underneath it!

Now we need to create a script that warps the party from Blamo's Dungeon to Blamo's Town. If we don't, the party enters the dungeon and can never return! Select "Create New Data" and go through the process again. Change the name to "Warp:BD to BT." Next, highlight the text box and select "Party," then "Teleport," then "Warp." Highlight "-None-" and this time select "Blamo's Town" from the menu. Select the placement icon and move the cursor to 90,125,0. This puts it right at our "Stairs Down" object. The yellow diamond is below land level, however. Press and hold L1 and the diamond rises, stopping automatically at ground level (90,125,2). Tap ✕ to update the black box, then exit to the main menu, remembering to update your data.

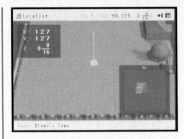

Make sure the yellow portion of the pointer is exactly where you want the party to appear.

CREATING A WARP EVENT

Okay, we've created our warp scripts, now we need to turn them into events. Select "Event" from the Scripts menu and you enter the Event database. Select "Create New Data" and rename the generic event to: "Warp:BT to BD." Although this event is tied to a model (the Stairs Down), do not select a "Model" here because we have already placed the Stairs Down object on the map.

NOTE

Earlier, we had you place the Stairs Down icon to help familiarize you with the object placement process. Because we knew all along that it would be an event (a warp in this case); we could have forgone that step and just selected "Stairs Down" within the "Model" field right here in the Event Editor. This would have linked the Stairs Down object with the "Warp:BT to BD" event and you could then place both at the same time (within the Event Placement Editor).

When you don't select a model for an event, the event appears as a transparent box for placement purposes, but is invisible when you play the game.

Now, make sure the "Start" field shows "Equal" to indicate that the event occurs when the party's location equals the event location. To finalize the event creation process, we have to apply the script. Move the cursor down to the "Apply" field and select "Warp:BT to BD" (remember that pressing R2 and L2 move the cursor up and down 10 scripts, respectively). Exit back to the Event database to create the last warp event.

Select "Create New Data" and change the name to "Warp:BD to BT." Keep "Model" set to "-None-" as we are not linking this warp to any object, character, or building. In the "Start" field select "Equal" to specify that the event is triggered when the character's location equals the event's location. Finally, move down to the "Apply" field and select "Warp:BD to BT" from the menu. Now both warp scripts have been successfully turned into events.

Both events have now been added to the Event database and are ready for placement.

PLACING THE WARP EVENTS

Now you need to place the events. From the main menu, select "Scripts," then "Event Placement." Look at the Event Placement database and notice that we have only created an Event Set for Blamo's Town (BT Events). We need to also create an Event Set for Blamo's Dungeon. Select "Create New Data" and change the generic Event Set name to "BD Events."

Then, move down to the "Dungeon Database" field and change "-None-" to "Blamo's Dungeon." Exiting now would create the Event Set, but we might as well place the warp event while we are here.

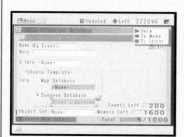

Now we've created an Event Set for Blamo's Dungeon called "BD Events." We can now place events within Blamo's Dungeon. Remember that we eventually need to register the Event Set in the World Organization database.

Select "Edit" and Blamo's Dungeon loads. We are now going to place the event "Warp:BD to BT" on the map. Move the cursor to coordinates 2,2,6 (you need to move the yellow box up using L1). This places the warp-to-town event behind where the party warps into the dungeon. If you had placed the event in front of their entrance point, the party would warp in, walk a few steps, and warp right back out!

Tap X and a blinking boat appears. Tap left on the directional pad once and "Warp:BD to BT" appears. Tap X to set the event. Now we need to place this event straight across the corridor so the party doesn't walk by it. Remember, we set the "Start" option to "equal," so the party must come in direct contact with the event to trigger it. Place the event three times all the way across the corridor, so the party cannot miss triggering it. Tap SELECT to exit the Event Placement Editor and return to the Event Placement database.

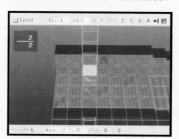

Placing event boxes across the corridor guarantees that the party triggers the event as they walk by.

REGISTERING THE BLAMO'S DUNGEON EVENT SET

Exit to the main menu and go to "Graphics," then "World Organization," and select "Blamo's Dungeon" from the database. Select "Edit," then change the "Events" field from "-None-" to "BD

Events." You have now activated all events that have been and will be placed on the map within the "BD Events" Event Set.

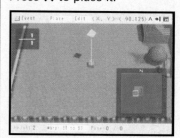

Remember, for an Object Set, Event Set, Unit Set, Background Music Set, or World Sounds Set to be active within a particular area, you must first select it within the World Organization Editor under the respective fields. For example, any event you place in Blamo's Dungeon will not work until you enter the World Organization database, select Blamo's Dungeon to edit, and pull up the Event Set you created for that dungeon. Once the Event Set is called up, any further events you place within that Event Set automatically activate.

Now we need to place the other warp event. Return to "Event Placement," select "BT Events" from the database, and select "Edit" from the menu. Move the cursor right to highlight and select the "Edit" button and Blamo's Town loads. Move the cursor directly over the Stairs Down (90,125) and tap X. Tap left on the directional pad until "Warp:BT to BD" appears. Press X to place it.

The warp event is activated when a party member steps on the stairs that lead down.

Test the game to make sure all is progressing well. The dialogue between Blamo and the Princess should be active, as should the warp from the stairs to Blamo's Dungeon and the warp back to town. If any of these events are broken, refer back to the appropriate section to fix them.

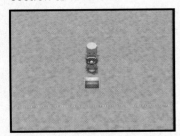

I step here...

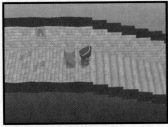

...and end up here!

ENEMY CREATION

A thief has stolen the Princess's ring, so we should create the thief.

ENEMY ACTIONS

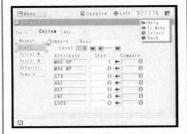

The Monster Action database contains more than 100 monsters, each with unique actions to copy or alter.

First, we create actions for our monster. Enter the Enemies menu and select "Enemy Actions." Highlight the "Enemy Action Database" and select "File 94:Dwarf." Select "Copy," then tap ● and select "Paste Copied Data." Change the name from "Dwarf" to "Thief" and exit to the main menu.

Never trust anyone who carries an axe bigger than himself.

NOTE

This is a beginner tutorial, so there is no need to create custom enemy actions. Just copy the "Dwarf" model and all the attacks associated with it.

ENTERING THE ENEMY IN THE ENEMY DATABASE

Now we need to enter the monster in the Enemy database. From the main menu, select "Enemies" twice, and the database pops up. Select "Create New Data" and change the generic name to "Jookie."

Jookie sounds like a good name for a thief.

CUSTOMIZING AN ENEMY'S STATS

At this point, our thief has no statistics.

Move down to the "Enemy Action" field and select your newly created "Thief" model. Notice that the Thief's "-Stats-" are lacking. Select the "Custom" tab and highlight the "Stats" sub-menu. In the "Compare" field, highlight "-None-" and tap ✗. Select "Captain Blamo" from the list of party members. You see a side-by-side comparison of Captain Blamo's stats and Jookie's stats (Make sure the "Level" field has "1" as a value). To create a simple, short battle, copy the values of Captain Blamo's stats into the "Stat" column for Jookie. But give Jookie double the "Max HP" of Blamo.

STAT COMPARISON

Attribute	Jookie's "Stat"	Blamo's "Compare" Stats
Max HP	50	24
Max MP	3	3
STR	11	11
AGI	5	5
DEF	10	10
INT	5	5
LUCK	10	10

That's better.

MAKING THE ENEMY ATTACK

Now Jookie can take a bit of damage from Blamo and Hooligan, but he won't fight back. To set Jookie to attack our heroes, highlight and select the "Adv" tab at the top of the page (next to "Custom").

This page allows you to set attacking and defending options for the enemy.

Once you have selected "Adv," move down the left set of sub-menus and select "Combat." Change the "Direct Effect" field to "0159:hit (Enemy 1)." This sets Jookie's to-hit percentage to 100 percent, and sets his damage to 5 (give or take 1 or 2 damage points due to his attributes).

Our guys can't take a lot, so make the thief more bark than bite.

CREATING A REWARD FOR DEFEATING THE ENEMY

This is where you set rewards for defeating enemies. Don't get greedy; we only came for the ring!

The final thing we need to set within the "Enemies" menu is the party's reward for defeating Jookie. Select the "Custom" tab and move the cursor down the left side until "Reward" is highlighted. Select the "Chest Ratio" field and change the ratio to "100." This makes the enemy cough up an item 100 percent of the time. Now, select the "Item Field" and select item "0093:Blessed Ring" from the list. Exit to the main menu, updating as you do so.

CREATING AN ENEMY UNIT

This is the Unit database. It has several groupings of monsters to work with.

Our next step is to set up our thief as a unit so we can tweak where and how he appears. Enter the "Unit" sub-menu from the "Enemies" menu. Select "Create New Data" and change the generic unit name to "Jookie." Now,

move down to the "Enemy" box and highlight "-None-" in the "1" field. Change "-None-" to Jookie and exit.

NOTE

Notice the option to choose up to four types of units and place them within one Unit Set. For example, we could have created an Undead unit comprising mummies and the like. We only want Jookie to appear, however, so he is set to both the enemy and the unit.

CREATING EVENTS WITH CONDITIONS

Now that our combatants are all ready, we need to set the place for the climatic final battle to occur.

CREATING A BATTLE SCRIPT

To create a battle script, we need to go into the "Scripts" menu, then the "Scripts" sub-menu and "Create New Data." Change the name of the script to "Thief Battle," then highlight the text box and tap X. Now, move down to "Other" and select "Event Battle" from the popup menu. Move the cursor up to the "Unit" field and select "Jookie."

The only way to specify an exact location for a fight is by selecting "Event Battle" from the Script Editor.

CREATING A BATTLE EVENT WITH CONDITIONS

Exit to the main menu and enter "Scripts," then "Events." Select "Create New Data" and change the name to "Thief Battle." Change the "Start" field to "Equal" and the "Apply" field to "0401:Thief Battle." Now your "Thief Battle" has been created. We need to tweak the event so it only occurs once, instead of every time you step on the event box. To do so, we make use of a feature called Page Condition.

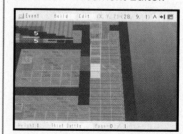

Page Conditions apply a script if certain preset conditions are met. You can set those conditions here.

Let's set a Page Condition. Within the Event Editor, with "Thief Battle" called up and ready to edit, select the "New" box at the top center of the screen. The "Page" field changes from "0" to "1" letting you know you are not altering your original data, which appears on page "0," but creating a new event condition.

Move the cursor to the "0" field and tap X; a menu pops up. Now check the bubble to the left of the "Has" field, the fifth field from the top. Within the "Has" field, select "-None-" and replace it with "0093:Blessed Ring."

You can choose what item the party must have to activate the event.

Finally, make sure that the "Apply" field has "-None-" listed. Basically, we just set a condition stating that if the party holds a certain item, the battle event does not recur the next time the party steps on the event box. Update your data and exit to the main menu.

PLACING THE BATTLE EVENT

Move into the "Event Placement" menu, select "BD Events" from the database and choose "Edit." Select the "Edit" button and Blamo's Dungeon loads. Move the cursor to 30,9,1 and tap X. Move the directional pad to the left and when "Thief Battle" appears, place the event by pressing X. Move straight across the floor, dropping two more "Thief Battle" event boxes the same way. Tap SELECT to exit the Event Placement Editor.

As we did with the warp event earlier, we need to make sure the party cannot avoid the event.

CREATING A DIALOGUE SCRIPT

We're almost done. It would be nice if the Princess acknowledged your hard work. So let's create a script to thank the party for recovering the stolen ring.

Enter the "Scripts" sub-menu from the "Scripts" main menu and select "Create New Data." Change the name to "Thanks" and select the large white text box. Now, choose: "Screen Display," "Text," then "Message." Finally, type: "Thank you, Blamo and Hooligan. You are my heroes!"

That's it? No kiss? Maybe we should keep the ring.

Okay, now we need to set up a Page Condition to apply the "Thanks" script when the party holds the Blessed Ring.

CREATING A DIALOGUE EVENT WITH CONDITIONS

Choose "Scripts" from the main menu, then "Events" to enter the Event database. Select "Greetings" from the list and choose to "Edit" it. Now, just as we did with the "Thief Battle" event, we want to create a new Page Condition. Select the "New" button and move down to the "0" field. Tap ✕ and select the "Has" button. Once again, change "-None-" to "Blessed Ring." Now change the following fields: "Display Type" should be "Character,

"Model" should be "Princess," "Start" should be "Talk," and "Apply" should be "Thanks." Now, when the party speaks with the Princess and they have the Blessed Ring in their possession, the "Thanks" script executes instead of the "Greetings" script.

This is how the Page Condition appears.

CONGRATULATIONS!

You did it! You created your first adventure. If you just went through the tutorial and followed the steps, without trying to understand what you were doing or how you were doing it, we suggest that you try to add to the adventure on your own, referring back to the tutorial only when needed. Try to place an NPC and create a greeting for it, or create a warp at the end of the dungeon that takes you directly back to town, or decorate the dungeon with a few objects.

Basically, get a feel for the flow of the menus and how they link together. When you begin to see the connections, read further and gain a more in-depth knowledge of each menu option.

SHARING YOUR GAME

Once you create your game, you can share it with your friends by copying the file to their memory card. Simply place your memory card in slot one, and your friend's card in slot two of the PS2. Boot up the system, select "Browser," and

select the file that contains the *RPG Maker* data. Select "Copy," then select "Memory Card (PS2)/2" and your game is saved to their card!

If you wish to share your game over the internet, there are peripheral devices that allow you to transfer games to your computer, then transfer them to players with similar devices. This is usually done via USB cable. Newer peripherals allow you to use the PS2 Broadband Adapter to transfer saved game files without additional cables or software. Take a look at Agetec's web site and check out their message boards for more information.

The party appears and speaks to the Princess. She has a quest for them.

The party accepts without hesitation.

Well, maybe they say no just once.

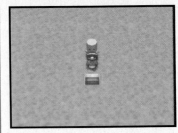

Who put stairs in the middle of this field?

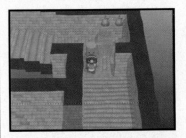

This looks more like a basement than a dungeon.

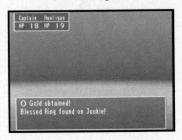

No experience or gold? Just a lousy ring!?

Maybe there would have been more of a reward if Blamo had been alone.

BASICS

If you completed the Sample Game Design in the previous chapter, you're familiar with the menus in *RPG Maker 2*. This section helps you understand what all the menus contain and why they are arranged as they are.

MENUS

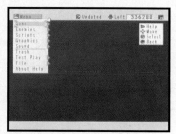

Eight menus are available for selection after you choose "New" or "Load" from the File menu. There is also a menu titled "About Help" that explains the Help system so generously included in the Region 1 version of this game (many thanks to the Agetec crew for taking pains to include this). Nearly 40 sub-menus are available from the eight main menu selections. Below, we give you a quick rundown of every sub-menu and what it's used for.

GAME

The Game menu includes many of the general options you need to specify when you start creating your game.

GAME SETTINGS: This menu includes general game settings, such as the ability to name your saved game file, change the look of the in-game text, specify the in-game camera angle, and alter the names of various statuses.

GENERAL SETTINGS: The General Settings menu allows you to specify your party, their starting items, and how often they encounter enemies.

PARTY MEMBERS: The Party Members menu includes the Party Member database, as well as many options you can use to customize how your characters advance through levels, how they act in battle, what equipment they begin the game with, and what resistances and vulnerabilities they have.

CLASSES: The Classes menu includes the Class database, and lets you alter everything related to character classes. Options include altering class names, prerequisites, statistics, and rewards.

TRAITS: The Traits menu includes the Trait database, and allows you to determine how an enemy or party member reacts in battle. Note that custom Traits are created with Script Commands, which need to be made before they are selected here.

ITEMS: The Item menu contains the Item database, which lists every item that appears in the game. You can also choose to create a new item and determine how the item is used, where it can be used, and what it does. If you create an item from scratch, you must pull its "effect" from the Direct Effects or Indirect Effects database to make it work.

ABILITIES: The Abilities menu includes the Ability database, which lists every spell and skill in the game. It also includes options to customize a pre-existing ability or create a new one. Like an item's effects, an ability's effects are pulled (or created from) the Direct Effects or Indirect Effects database.

DIRECT EFFECTS: The Direct Effects menu includes the Direct Effect database. Direct Effects are non-lingering effects that occur immediately upon usage (a potion, for example) or upon a successful hit (weapon damage). Creating Direct Effects from scratch is recommended for advanced users only.

INDIRECT EFFECTS: The Indirect Effects menu includes the Indirect Effects database. Indirect Effects are any effects that have duration. A Sleep spell or a damage-over-time poison are examples of Indirect Effects. Direct and Indirect Effects can be applied to weapons, items, and abilities.

ENEMIES

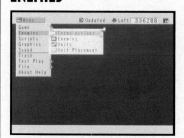

The Enemies menu has just about everything you need to alter or create a unique enemy.

NOTE

The order of creating an enemy is identical to the order of the sub-menus within the Enemies menu (Enemy Actions, Enemies, Units, Unit Placement). If you wish to create a unique model for your enemy, visit the Enemy Models sub-menu within the Graphics menu first.

ENEMY ACTIONS: The Enemy Actions menu includes the Enemy Action database and the Enemy Action Editor. The Editor allows you to create custom enemy animations from pre-existing actions.

ENEMIES: The Enemies menu includes the Enemy database, which lists every enemy in the game. You can also set the enemy's statistics, resistances, and behaviors, and the experience and loot reward for killing that enemy.

UNITS: The Unit menu includes the Units database, and the ability to set any number of enemies into specific units. For example, you can create a unit of all undead creatures and have them appear together on the map. You can also test your party against that unit for balancing purposes.

UNIT PLACEMENT: Here you add all the units that appear on a certain map. You can also individually set how often each unit appears. For example, rare monsters can be set to appear only five percent of the time.

As you move through the menus, notice that the three most recently selected menus appear on top of the pulldown menu. This allows you to move back to those menus a little faster.

SCRIPTS

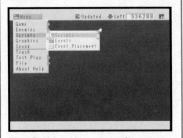

The Scripts menu contains everything you need to create scripts and events. Individual Script Commands make up scripts, and scripts make up events. Every time the party interacts with anything, be it a treasure box or an NPC, an event is involved. Understanding scripts and events is key to becoming an advanced user.

SCRIPTS: The Script database includes almost 400 scripts. The scripts direct all the events in the game, and are called up in certain menus to do everything from directing battle flow to directing an NPC's actions. You can alter or create scripts to suit your needs.

EVENTS: The Event menu includes the Event database, which comprises more than 350 events. Events are used every time your character interacts, attacks, moves, or is given on-screen information. The Event Editor lets you create an event from custom or pre-existing scripts.

EVENT PLACEMENT: This is where you place existing or custom events on your World, Town, or Dungeon maps.

GRAPHICS

The Graphics menu consists of model databases, creation editors, and tools to create visual effects, place objects, and organize all your pieces.

CHARACTER MODELS: The Character Models menu includes the Character Models database, which consists of more than 100 models you can use to populate your world. You can customize the models in a variety of ways.

OBJECT MODEL: The Object Model menu includes the Object Model database, which consists of 264 items, objects, and buildings to decorate your world, town, or dungeon. You can also alter the appearance of your object in the Object Editor.

ENEMY MODELS: This menu includes the Enemy Model database, which allows you to choose and alter any of the 100 or so enemy models available.

NOTE

The appendices near the end of this guide include thumbnails of every character, object, and enemy for quick reference.

BUILDING EDITOR: The Building Editor allows you to construct buildings from scratch. You can then customize your creation with the use of more than 400 textures.

DUNGEON EDITOR: The Dungeon Editor allows you to create custom dungeons and interiors for your game. As with the Building Editor, you can customize your dungeon with the use of textures.

MAP EDITOR: Use the Map Editor to create the foundation

upon which your adventure is built. You can create rolling hills, snowcapped mountains, small ponds, and vast oceans. You can then add grass and trees to the land, or change the light depending on the time of day.

NOTE

Thumbnails of all textures are included near the end of this guide for your visual reference.

OBJECT PLACEMENT: Enter the Object Placement menu to create an Object Set that consists of all the objects you place on a particular map. Once you name your Object Set and place all the objects on a given map, your Object Set appears in the Object Placement database. You then need to register the Object Set in World Organization. You create a different Object Set for each map (dungeon, world, town) you want to place objects upon.

WORLD ORGANIZATION: This is where all the pieces come together. Within World Organization, you select a map and link it to the Object Set, Event Set, and Unit Set you created in their respective menus. You can also choose background music and world sound effects for your map. You create a World Set for each map you create.

VISUAL EFFECTS: Choose from more than 150 visual effects to use or alter within the Visual Effects database. The Visual Effects Editor is a great tool to create custom visual effects.

IMAGE: Pull an image from certain digital cameras, provided they have specific software installed. See the instruction manual for more information.

NOTE

RPG Maker 2 comes with a screenshot function that allows you to take and use in-game screenshots for use as visual effects. To take a screenshot, press the right analog button (R3) and the left analog button (L3), then access it by selecting "Graphics/Image/Create New Data/ Get/Screenshot Image." Only the last screenshot is saved.

SOUND TEST

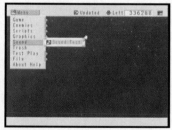

You can listen to all of RPG Maker 2's music and sound effects within the Sound Test menu. You can also test the Volume, Pitch, and Tempo functions within the game.

TRASH

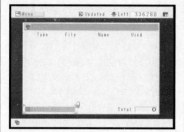

When you delete something within RPG Maker 2, it ends up in the Trash. Visit the Trash menu to find out where deleted items are used, or to empty the Trash and free up memory.

TIP

Press SELECT while working within a menu to minimize it and get back to the main menu. Two things happen when this is done: an "open-book" icon appears next to the menu you just exited and an icon of the editor will appear at the bottom of the menu screen (shortcut bar) that allows you to open the menu back up. The shortcut bar can be accessed by pressing the directional pad down when your cursor is on the "Menu" button. Selecting an open menu icon will take you back to where you were working when you pressed SELECT. Use this function to move quickly between multiple menus.

TEST PLAY

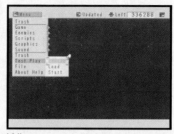

When you want to test your adventure, select "Test Play," then "Start." You can also load saved Test Play data by selecting "Load."

NOTE

While in Test Play, access the Debug menu by tapping ✕ and selecting "Debug." This is an extremely helpful menu that allows you to switch Flags on or off, access and enter numbers and text into Variables, and start Events for testing purposes. You can also Quick Save the game so you can begin again where you left off (Select Test Play/Load).

FILE

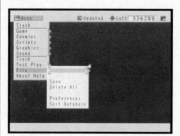

Use the File menu to save, delete, and load data, as well as to change the difficulty level and sort the databases.

NEW: Select this option to begin a new game. Then select a difficulty level for your game.

LOAD: Use this option to load previously saved data.

SAVE: Select this to save your data. Remember, updating your data does not permanently save it. Select the "Save" option to ensure your data is saved to the Memory Card.

DELETE ALL: Select this to erase all your updated data. Delete All must be performed before you can load new data or return to the title screen.

TITLE SCREEN: Select this to return to the title screen.

PREFERENCES: Select this option to change the difficulty level or change the editing environment. You can, for example, select a different background or change the volume of the in-game music. You can also set how quickly (if at all) you would like the Operation Guide to appear.

SORT DATABASE: Select any database in the game and move the entries around to suit your preference.

TIP

To save a lot of time, plan your adventure before you start creating. List all the objects (non-events) and events, and script out the dialogue and on-screen messages. Finally, create a list of party members and NPCs. Do this for each map you wish to create. A bit of forethought eliminates the redundancies inherent in the creation process.

GAME SETTINGS

In the Game Settings menu, you can customize many of the default settings that are applied throughout the course of your adventure. Explore these options—from naming your saved game to setting the angle of the in-game camera—to add personal touches to your adventure.

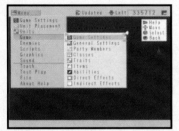

Enter the Game Settings page by selecting "Game," then "Game Settings" from the main menu.

THE BASIC PAGE

Enter the Text Input screen and choose "Game Name" and "Designer" to produce a file name to be used when saving. Neither appears as a title screen. See "Scripts and Event Creation" for details on how to create a title screen.

THE CUSTOM PAGE

The Custom page allows you to customize many in-game options, such as text color, camera control, and naming conventions.

WINDOWS

The Windows page allows you to alter the default text box that appears throughout the game, as well as change text colors to your liking.

STYLE: Select either a "Framed" or "Beveled" look for your text boxes. The "Preview" pane reflects either choice when they are selected.

BORDER: Select the "Border" color for your text box.

BACKGROUND: Select up to four background colors for your text box. The colors you select fill different parts of the box and blend where multiple colors meet. Be careful—loud colors may make it hard to read like-colored text within the box.

TRANS: If you chose bright colors for your background, increase the transparency percentage so text shows up more clearly.

PAGE: The left color box sets the color of the "next page" arrow that appears when there are multiple pages of text onscreen. The right color box selects the color of the page arrow's shadow.

TEXT SWATCH: Tap START over the various color boxes to see what, if anything, that particular color denotes in-game. Change the colors as you see fit.

NOTE

You can change the color and size of particular messages or lines of dialogue by creating a script. Enter the Script Editor by selecting "Scripts," then "Scripts" from the main menu. Select "Create New Data," then select "Screen Display," "Text," and "Color and Size." See "Script and Event Creation" for more information.

CAMERA

Go to the Camera page to set the default viewpoint angle for the camera.

TIP

Choosing a low angle makes your party appear much larger than a higher angle does, but it also limits your field of vision. It's possible to keep the default camera angle and change the camera angle at specific times during the game for stylistic flair. Do this with a Script Command.

SFX

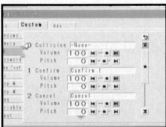

The SFX or Sound Effects page allows you to choose sound effects for certain actions within the game. You can choose from among 200 sound effects and vary each sound's pitch, allowing for almost limitless customization.

PASSWORD

Check the "Enable Password" box to set a password to protect your data. If you forget your password, you can never retrieve your data. It might be best to just hide your Memory Card from your little sister.

MENU TEXT

Change the default action names here to anything you like. For example, change "Talk" to "Converse." As with many other options, individual action names can be called up using scripts. To call up a name, use "Screen Display/Content/Menu Text" within the Script Editor.

SEX

Customize here what you want to call different genders. You can then call up your custom name within the Party Member Editor ("Game/Party Members/Custom/Detail").

PROPERTY W/PROPERTY M

These two pages allow you to change the names for various weapon and magic properties. They correspond to the resistances set within the Member and Enemy Editors.

FLAG

Change flag names here. Flags are switches that are either "On" or "Off," "Yes" or "No." Has a chest been opened? Yes. Can it be opened again? No. Is the party engaged in a battle? Yes. Custom flags are turned on and off within the Enemy

Editor, the Party Members Editor, and within General Settings. They can also be altered with a Script Command (Select "Data/Flags" within the Script Editor).

VARIABLE

Setting variables allows you to call up a particular variable at any point in the game using Script Commands. You can then use that variable for just about anything. For example, the Help menu mentions a bank account balance, so let's use that. Within the Party Member Editor, set "NormalVariable0" to equal 16. Then change the name of "NormalVariable0" to "Age." Finally, set up a Script Command that makes the banker give the party 16 gold (one for each year, as a reward for opening an account). To create a script like this, enter the Script Editor and use "Data/Variable."

INPUT

Inputs are the alphabetic equivalent of variables. They call up words rather than numbers. You can name the input variables here and use them in the same places and ways that we discussed earlier for variables. Within the Script Editor, select "Data/Input" to alter a certain input.

THE ADVANCED PAGE

The Advanced page allows you to customize the way battles play out, and set names for various statuses.

NOTE

The intermediate user does not need to tweak most of these options. Until you become familiar with scripts and events, leave most of these settings as they are.

SETTINGS

The Settings page allows you to change the event settings for various in-game actions.

SYSTEM: Changing this event modifies how various errors are called out within the game.

WORLD DEATH: If the party is killed on the World Map, this event determines what happens.

DEAD: This event determines how a party wipe-out is handled both on the World Map and within battle. It allows you to return to your previous save point.

ENTER/EXIT MAP: Set an event here to handle entering and exiting a map. These events are overruled by events called up in "World Organization/Script."

DEATH INDIRECT: This tells the game how to handle the indirect effect of death. You can customize this by selecting "Death" from the Indirect Effects database within "Game/Indirect Effects."

■ BUTTON: This binds an event to the ■ button. The default event is "Debug Menu;" change that before letting others play your game.

CAMERA

The Camera page allows for more camera customization than "Custom/Camera" does.

WORLD/BATTLE: Change both the angle (down to the degree) and the distance of the camera on the World Map and in battle.

NOTE

If you increase the camera distance, you increase by 50 percent the allotted room to place enemies within "Enemies/Units/Basic." For example, if you increase the distance by 100, you get 50 more units of space to place enemies. Decreasing the distance decreases the space by the same percentage.

USER MENU

Create a custom in-game user menu by selecting an event within at least one of the 10 fields. Use this to give members special abilities. Once you become adept with scripts, you can customize the abilities to have limitations such as "only used once per day."

BATTLE 1/BATTLE 2

These pages allow you to customize how battles play out. It's wise to leave these settings alone until you are well experienced with the minutiae of script and event creation.

ACTION

Set enemy action names here. They are not displayed in-game, but you may want to come here and change the generic names after you have created custom actions in the Enemy Action Editor.

CONDITION/MAGIC/SKILL

Like the Action page, the Condition, Magic, and Skill pages allow you to change the names of the respective lines.

WORLD CREATION

USING THE MAP EDITOR

The Map Editor is used to create the land upon which your adventure occurs. From snow-covered mountain ranges to dense forests, you can create a world that fits your unique story. What follows is a tutorial on how to use the basic editing controls. With a little work, you can create just about any type of topography you can imagine.

NOTE

Below are the controls for Normal and Hard difficulty.

BASIC CONTROLS

Action	Command
Create/Edit/Place	✕
Cancel	●
Exit Map Editor	SELECT
Display help text	START
Move cursor	Directional pad ↑/↓/←/→
Switch to Edit mode	■ + directional pad ↑
Switch to Copy mode	■ + directional pad ←
Switch to Delete mode	■ + directional pad ↓
Switch to Paste mode	■ + directional pad →
Switch to Build mode	■ + L2
Switch to Texture mode	■ + L1
Switch to Confirm mode	■ + R2
Switch to View (edit-all) mode	■ + R1
Toggle between A/B data	■ + L3
Quick-move cursor	R2 + directional pad ↑/↓/←/→
Change window transparency	▲ + R1
Hide/unhide windows	▲ + R2
Toggle Stop/Free cursor mode	▲ + L1
Jump to next pointer	L2 + R2 + directional pad ↑/↓/←/→
Undo/redo one time	R1 + R2 + ●

NOTE

Press R1 + R2 + L1 + L2 + ✕ while in Delete mode to delete all.

PASTE MODE

Action	Command
Flip	▲ + directional pad ↑/↓/←/→
Rotate 90 degrees	▲ + rotate left analog stick
Back to default	▲ + L3

BUILD MODE

Action	Command
Change height	L1 / L2
Resize area horizontally/vertically	directional pad ↑/↓/←/→
Toggle between build methods	▲ + directional pad ↑
Switch the terrain shape	▲ + directional pad ↓
Rotate terrain	▲ + directional pad ←/→
Rotate terrain 45 degrees	■ + L1
Toggle between heights	■ + L2
Toggle between slope angles	■ + R1
Toggle between peak shapes	■ + R2
Change slope	■ + directional pad ↑/↓
Change peak shape	■ + directional pad ←/→

TEXTURE MODE

Action	Command
Select texture	L1 / L2
Resize area	directional pad ↑/↓/←/→
Toggle between blending methods	▲ + directional pad ↑
Switch the landscape shape	▲ + directional pad ↓
Rotate texture area	▲ + directional pad ←/→
Rotate texture area 45 degrees	■ + L1
Select landscape from three types	■ + L2
Toggle between transparency	■ + R1
Toggle between edge blending	■ + R2
Change transparency	■ + directional pad ↑/↓
Change edge blending	■ + directional pad ←/→

CAMERA OPERATION

Action	Command
Change view	R1 + directional pad ↑/↓/←/→
Rotate view	R1 + L1/L2
Zoom view	R1 + rotate left analog stick
Toggle between zoom amounts	R1 + left analog button L3

OVERVIEW MAP OPERATION

Action	Command
Change size	R1 + rotate right analog stick
Toggle between sizes	R1 + R3

LIGHT SOURCE OPERATION

Action	Command
Move light source	R1 + R2 + directional pad ↑/↓/←/→
Back to default	R1 + R2 + L2

WHEN EDITING (CURSOR ON A POINTER)

Action	Command
Place another pointer	R1 + ✕
Set lowest priority to selected pointer	▲ + L2 + directional pad ↑
Set highest priority to selected pointer	▲ + L2 + directional pad ↓
Lower priority of selected pointer by 1	▲ + L2 + directional pad ←
Raise priority of selected pointer by 1	▲ + L2 + directional pad →
Toggle between pointers currently selected	L1/L2

CONFIRM MODE

Action	Command
Move character	directional pad ↑/↓/←/→
Move character and ignore collisions	● + directional pad ↑/↓/←/→
Change character	▲ + directional pad ↑/↓/←/→
Toggle between times of day	R1 + R2 + L1 + directional pad ↑/↓
Select next weather type	R1 + R2 + R3
Change weather amounts	R1 + R2 + L1 + directional pad ←/→

LET THERE BE LAND

Enter the Map database by selecting "Graphics," then "Map Editor" from the main menu. Select "Create New Data," then the "Basic" tab. Change the generic map name to something more personal, then select the "Edit" button to begin creating.

Tap ✕ and a circular piece of land appears. Because the overhead view makes it difficult to see the land's shape, look at the semi-transparent box that sits in the northwest portion of the screen. You can see from the simple graphic display that the land actually has a slight slope and a low peak.

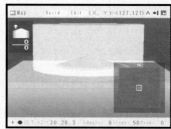

Make use of the camera to periodically check the shape of the created terrain by holding R2 and pressing the directional pad in the desired direction. From a better vantage point, you can confirm the slight conical shape of the land.

Because you haven't pressed ✕ again to confirm the land placement, you can still alter the shape of the land. Move the directional pad left and the land is condensed vertically. Condense it enough and the slope becomes great enough to form a cliff face.

NOTE

Pressing up on the directional pad condenses the land horizontally.

Hold the directional pad right to spread the land back out. Now press L2 to raise the elevation of the land. A snowcap automatically forms if you raise the land to a certain elevation above sea level.

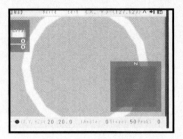

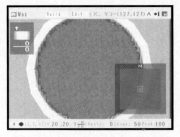

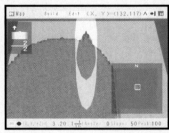

Conversely, holding L2 lowers the elevation of the land, all the way down to sea level. At this elevation, the land is covered by water.

To decrease the elevation, press L2. Decrease the elevation to just above sea level and you notice the land no longer resembles a hill, as it did when we first started, but rather a plateau, perfect for placing a town.

Let's make the northern side of our square a mountainous region. Move the pointer to coordinates 127,17 (the X,Y coordinates can be found at the top of the screen). Tap X once to enter Edit mode. Change the shape of the land by pressing ▲ + the directional pad down. Notice the unnatural cliff faces that appear. This is due to the build mode we are in.

Move the cursor to 132,17 and tap X. Now, condense the land's shape by pressing left on the directional pad. Very little happens to the shape. No high peaks are created, nor any cliffs.

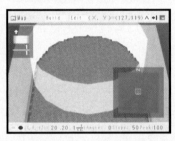

Press and hold ■ + tap L2 to quickly change the elevation from an underwater canyon, to sea level, to a snowcapped mountain. Leave the land as a snowcapped mountain.

Before we confirm our land placement, try pressing ▲ + the directional pad down. This changes the overall land shape to a square. Although the square looks unnatural, it provides us with a larger surface area to work with. Tap X to place the land.

Look at the bottom left corner of the HUD. Do you see the "+" symbol? The "+" symbol indicates that new terrain is added to the old terrain. In this case, the "new" section is placed on top of the already created land, and you get an elevated region. To change building methods, press ▲ + the directional pad up. The "+" will change to an "=" symbol indicating that any new terrain placed over existing terrain takes priority, and the old terrain is removed. Tap L2 to bring the new terrain level with the old terrain (you may have to bring it back up with L1 if the upper portion sinks too low). Tap X to place your second piece of land.

Change the building method back to "+" by pressing ▲ + the directional pad up. A mountainous region is created.

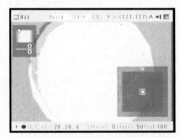

Press and hold ■ + the directional pad right to increase the angle of the slope all the way up to vertical. Notice that the land becomes a thick, snow-covered pancake. This is because only the slope changed, not the elevation.

Your first piece of land has been placed, and a faded yellow marker marks the center of your creation. If you wish to re-edit a particular piece of land, place the pointer over the marker and tap X. This selects the already placed land for re-editing.

To make the new region hug the coast, rotate the terrain by pressing ▲ + left on the directional pad. You can also release ▲ and use the directional pad to condense or expand the land until it looks more natural, rather than like a strip of mountains dropped on a perfectly flat piece of land.

To create the snowcapped appearance, press [L1] until the elevation rises sufficiently, and the snow appears. Play with changing the slope (■ + directional pad up/down) and peak shape (■ + directional pad left/right) until you are happy with the look of your mountain.

Try creating another mountain next to the previous one to create the look of a mountain range. Make sure the build mode is set to "=" (▲ + directional pad up) so the new mountain doesn't engulf the old one.

You can create peaks by condensing a circular terrain shape (toggle terrain shapes by pressing ▲ + directional pad down) and raising the elevation ([L1]). Manipulating the slope and peak shape also adds to your creation.

NOTE

The more time you spend messing around in the Map Editor, the easier it becomes to create complex landscapes, and the more realistic the landscapes appear.

TEXTURES

Even with our mountains, the land looks plain. It would be nice to add some color or even a forest to our little world. That is where textures come in. After you have laid the groundwork, look to textures to add the finishing touches.

Let's add a forest next to our mountain range. To enter Texture mode, press ■ + [L1]. Notice that the transparent display switches from a graphical view of the land to a patch of grass with the word "Texture" overlaid.

Tap ✕ next to the mountain range and the texture selection box appears. The green default texture fills the editing area.

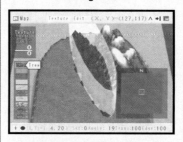

Tap [L1]/[L2] to select from the various textures. After you have browsed through them, settle on the top texture, labeled "Tree." A forest overruns your mountain range; it looks like we have some editing to do.

Use the same area editing techniques you used while creating terrain. Using the directional pad condenses and expands the forest, while pressing ▲ + directional pad left/right rotates the texture. You may also need to cancel the placement with ● and place the pointer somewhere else.

Place the forest next to the mountains, then condense and rotate it until it looks like a nice strip. Repeat the process a few times and you'll have a nice-looking forest.

Finally, throw some grass on the dirt to give the world a more hospitable feel. Place the pointer at the southern end of the land and tap ✕. Because we created a square piece of land, change the landscape shape from circular to square by pressing ▲ + the directional pad down. Now, select the third texture from the top. Rotate it and condense or expand it until it covers the land. Tap ✕ to finalize the process.

ADVANCED EDITING TECHNIQUES

The "Basic" page includes the "B Data" field. To use B Data, highlight the field and press ✕. Select a custom or pre-existing map that you want to use for B Data. After you enter the editor, you can access B Data by pressing ■ + the left analog button ([L3]). Copy what you want from the B Data, then press ■ + the left analog button to return to the editor. Now paste the B Data and manipulate it as you desire. Note that B Data is not saved, so don't create anything on the B side as it will be lost when you exit the editor. Use B Data to take pieces of maps, dungeons, or buildings (depending on which editor you are in) for use in new creations.

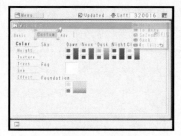

The "Custom" Tab includes many useful features to further customize your map.

COLOR

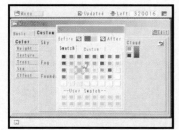

Change the colors in the "Sky" field to specify the color of the sky at dawn, noon, dusk, night, and when it's cloudy. Change the colors within the "Fog" and "Foundation" field to alter the colors when fog is present, and the non-rendered area of the map.

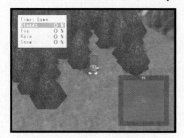

To see how these changes play out, select the "Edit" button to load up your map. Now, enter Confirm mode by pressing ■ + R2. To toggle through time periods, press R1 + R2 + L1 + the directional pad up/down. To add clouds, tap left and right while pressing R1 + R2 + L1. To cycle through the weather selections, press R1 + R2 + L1 + right analog button R3.

HEIGHT

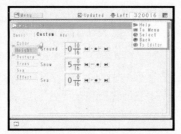

The "Height" tab allows you to set ground level, sea level, and the altitude at which snow automatically appears on your terrain.

TIP

Lower the "Snow" value to create a snow-covered map. Raise it if you want little or no snow to appear on your map.

TEXTURE

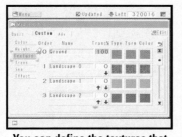

You can define the textures that appear on your land on the "Texture" page. Eleven land textures are available to alter, as well as a snow texture, two slope textures, and two sea textures.

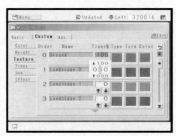

Use the "Trans%" field to further alter the look of your terrain. If you

change the transparency percentage, terrain types stacked on top of each other have a different look.

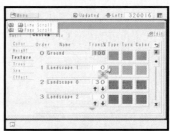

Select the priority order of your terrain types by using the arrow buttons in the "Trans%" column. The terrain type with the highest priority is stacked on top of a terrain type of lower priority. Lower the transparency percentage and the lower terrain begins to show through the upper terrain.

TREES

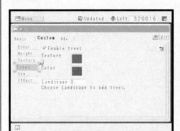

The "Trees" page allows you to customize the texture and color of your trees. You can also set trees to be applied automatically when you place a certain landscape.

SEA

The "Sea" page allows you to customize the look of the sea. You can choose the color, type, texture, and transparency of your sea here. You can even alter the look of the sea at different times of the day.

EFFECTS

The "Effects" page includes tools to alter the type and amount of light and shadow that appear on your map. Play with the color palette within the "Sun" and "Light" fields to create fantastic atmospheric lighting. Increase or decrease the "Ratio" field to alter the amount of light that appears. The "Shadow" fields allow you to change the density of the shadows and the "Range" field allows you to set the length of your shadows.

To view the effects of the sun, light, and shadow variables, select "Edit," then enter Confirm mode once your map loads (■ + R2). Toggle through times of the day by pressing R1 + R2 + L1 plus the directional pad up/down.

ADVANCED/SEA

Select the "Adv" tab to customize the attributes of the sea.

NOTE

That's all there is to it! Experiment with the textures to create everything from sand to lava. Try creating forests that are less dense, then placing a fill texture below it. As with land creation, the more time you spend experimenting, the better you become.

USING THE DUNGEON AND BUILDING EDITORS

The Dungeon and Building Editors use the same controls, so refer to the following tables when you are working in either editor.

NOTE

Below are the controls for the Normal and Hard difficulty levels.

BASIC ACTIONS

Action	Command
Create/Edit/Place	✕
Cancel	●
Exit Editor	SELECT
Display help text	START
Move cursor X and Y axis	directional pad ↑/↓/←/→
Move cursor Z axis	L1/L2
Switch to Edit (Build) mode	■ + directional pad ↑
Switch to Copy mode	■ + directional pad ←
Switch to Delete mode	■ + directional pad ↓
Switch to Paste mode	■ + directional pad → (Only after Copy mode)
Switch to Texture mode	■ + L1
Switch to View mode	■ + R1
Switch to Transparency mode	■ + L2
Switch to Confirm mode	■ + R2

BASIC ACTIONS CONTINUED

Action	Command
Toggle between A/B data	■ + L3
Change window transparency	▲ + R1
Hide/unhide windows	▲ + R2
Toggle Stop/Free cursor mode	▲ + L1
Undo/redo one time	R1 + R2 + ●

NOTE

To delete all: press R1 + R2 + L1 + L2 + ✕ while in Delete mode.

PASTE MODE

Action	Command
Flip X axis	▲ + rotate left analog stick
Flip Y axis	▲ + L3

BUILD MODE

Action	Command
Select block shape	▲ + directional pad ←/→
Rotate block direction	▲ + rotate left analog stick
Flip block up/down	▲ + L3
Sample block at cursor	▲ + L2
Turn on/off block transparency	▲ + directional pad ↑/↓
Change block texture	R2 + directional pad ↑/↓/←/→
Toggle between upper/lower textures	R2 + L1
Copy texture	R2 + L3
Paste texture	R2 + R3
Flip texture	R2 + L2 + directional pad ↑/↓
Rotate texture	R2 + rotate left analog stick
Place current texture on all sides of block	R2 + L2 + L3

CAMERA OPERATION

Action	Command
Change view	R2 + directional button ↑/↓/←/→
Rotate view 180 degrees	R1 + L1/L2
Zoom view	R1 + rotate left analog stick
Toggle between zoom amounts	R1 + L3

LIGHT SOURCE OPERATION

Action	Command
Move light source	R1 + R2 + directional buttons ↑/↓/←/→
Back to default	R1 + R2 + L1

CONFIRM MODE

Action	Command
Move character	directional pad ↑/↓/←/→
Move character and ignore collisions	● + directional pad ↑/↓/←/→
Change character	● + directional pad ↑/↓/←/→
Select next weather type (Dungeon Editor only)	R1 + R2 + R3
Change weather amounts (Dungeon Editor only)	R1 + R2 + L1 + directional pad ←/→

While in Build/Edit mode, press ▲ + L2 to quick-copy the block shape and texture of the block your cursor is highlighting.

CREATING A DUNGEON FROM SCRATCH

The Dungeon Editor is used to create both dungeons and interiors. We take you through the creation process step by step so you can get the hang of it. We also texture the dungeon so it looks more like a dungeon. We finish the chapter by looking at some advanced editing techniques that you can play with after you master the basics.

Enter the Dungeon database by selecting "Graphics" from the main menu, then selecting "Dungeon Editor." As we are creating a dungeon from scratch, select the "Create New Data" button and the "Dungeon Editor" pops up. Select the "Basic" tab, then highlight and select the "Name" field by pressing ✕. Using either a USB keyboard or the on-screen controls, enter a name for your dungeon. When finished, exit the Text Input screen by pressing ●. Update and save your data. Highlight and select the "Edit" button to the right of the "Custom" tab. You are now able to create a dungeon.

A FLOOR AND FOUR WALLS

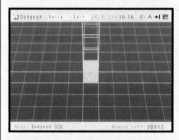

You are presented with a yellow-lined grid and a cursor that looks like a wire-framed column. The solid yellow cube that represents the shape of the block you are about to place rests at coordinates 16,16,0.

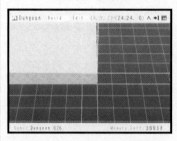

Tap ✕ once and a block is placed. Tap the control pad right until the coordinates read 24,16,0. A line of yellow blocks should trail the cursor. Move the directional pad down until you hit coordinates 24,24,0. Tap ✕ and the floor is set.

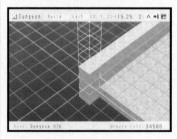

Let's outline our floor with a wall. Move the cursor to 15,15,0 and tap ✕. Now, press L1 twice to raise the elevation. Tap the directional pad down until the coordinates read 15,25,2. Tap ✕ and your first wall is set.

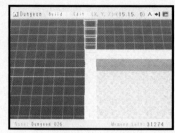

Outline the rest of the floor with walls in the same way. To change the camera angle, press and hold R1 while tapping the directional buttons. This makes it easier to see where the cursor is located, relative to the floor.

STAIRS

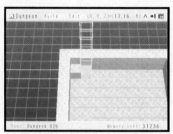

Let's make some stairs. Move the cursor to 16,16,1 and place a single block by tapping ✕ twice. Move the cursor right one space (17,16,1) and press and hold ▲. The different block shapes pop up. While holding ▲, move the directional pad left once to highlight the block that is 75 percent the size of the default block. Release ▲ and the yellow cursor reflects the new block size.

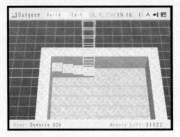

Place the block by pressing ✕ twice. Move the cursor to the right one space to coordinates 18,16,1. Press and hold ▲ and highlight the next block to the left. Release ▲ and place the block by tapping ✕ twice. Repeat the process once more with the thinnest block and you have your set of stairs.

NOTE

A character can only move up or down steps that are 25 percent higher or lower than the one he or she is on.

TEXTURES

There are two ways to texture your dungeon. The first is to enter Texture mode; the second is to texture your blocks as you place them. Because we have already created the dungeon, we start off by texturing in Texture mode.

TEXTURE MODE

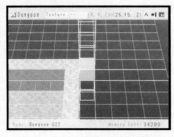

The gray color is boring, so let's dress up our dungeon. Move the cursor to coordinates 26,15,0 and press and hold ■ + ⌊L1⌋. The cursor color should change to a light blue to indicate you have entered Texture mode.

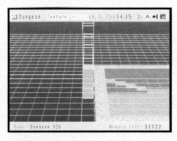

Tap ✕ to set the starting point for your texture. Move the cursor along the wall to coordinates 14,15,2, but do not press ✕ again. Now, hold ⌊R1⌋ and tap the directional pad up and down until you are facing the inside of the wall (the side you want to texture).

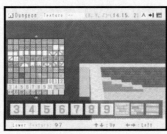

Press and hold ⌊R2⌋ and highlight Texture #97. You notice that the wall changes as you move through the different textures. Release ⌊R2⌋ and the front face of the wall takes on the selected texture. Tap ✕ once again to set the texture.

NOTE

The side of the wall that is textured depends on the position of the camera before you push ⌊R2⌋ and highlight a texture. Basically, only the side of the wall that the camera is facing receives the texture.

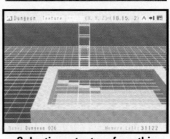

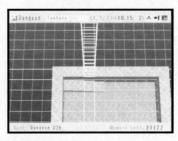

Selecting a texture from this angle textures only the front of the wall.

Selecting a texture from this angle textures only the top of the wall.

It's tricky, and it takes some camera manipulation skills, but you'll get the hang of it soon enough.

NOTE

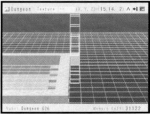

To texture the inside of the western wall, move the cursor to 15,14,2. Remember to change the camera angle so you are looking directly at the inside of the wall.

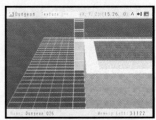

Tap ✕ and move the cursor to coordinates 15,26,0. Press and hold ⌊R2⌋, then highlight Texture #97. The inside of the wall takes on the texture. Release ⌊R2⌋ and tap ✕ to set the texture.

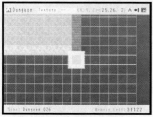

Finish texturing the inside of the last two walls, then texture the tops of all the walls. Remember, to texture the top of a wall, you must be facing it (move the camera until you are looking straight down on the wall).

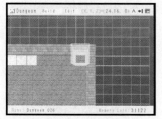

Texture the floor the same way you textured the tops of the walls. Move the cursor to coordinates 24,16,0 and use [R1] + the directional pad to position the camera above the floor.

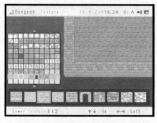

Tap ✕ to set the start point, then move the cursor to coordinates 16,24,0. Press and hold [R2] and highlight Texture

#112. Release [R2] and tap ✕ to set the texture.

NOTE

One drawback of Texture mode is not being able to see the cursor when you select portions of a wall of floor. For example, if you followed the last two steps, you couldn't tell whether or not the area was being selected when you moved the cursor to coordinates 16,24,0. However, pressing [R2] only brings up the texture selection screen if you have selected an area to be textured. If you press [R2] and the selection screen does not pop up, you forgot to tap ✕ to set a start point.

You should be able to texture the stairs on your own. Just remember, the camera must be facing the area you wish to texture. Try texturing the tops and sides of the stairs differently.

TEXTURING WHILE CREATING

Instead of erasing all your hard work and starting from scratch, let's just re-texture a wall or two without entering Texture mode.

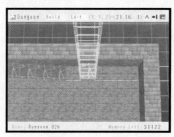

Press ■ + directional pad up to leave Texture mode and enter the default Build/Edit mode. Recall that anytime you press ✕ in this mode, a block is placed.

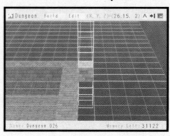

Move the cursor to coordinates 25,15,2. Now, use [R1] and the directional pad to change the camera angle so that it points at the inside face of the yellow cursor cube. Press and hold [R1] and highlight Texture #98. Release [R1] and you see that the side of the cube the camera was facing changed to the new texture.

NOTE

Texture is only placed on the side of the cube that the camera is facing at the time of texture selection. This lets you place different textures on all six sides of the cube.

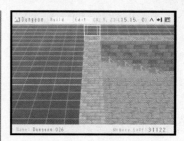

Tap ✕ and move the cursor to coordinates 15,15,0. Tap ✕ again and the wall's texture changes.

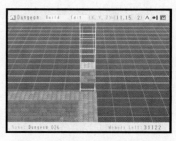

Placing textures on the other walls entails placing textures on the other sides of the yellow cube. Move the cursor to coordinates 11,15,2 and press and hold [R1]. Now tap the directional pad to the right two times. Notice that the face of the yellow cube you are now viewing doesn't reflect a texture. Press and hold [R2], and select Texture #98. Release [R2] and that problem is solved.

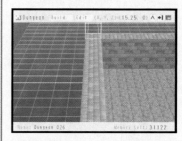

Move the cursor to coordinates 15,15,2, and tap ✕ to set the starting point for your textured wall. Now move the cursor to 15,25,0 and press ✕ to fully texture the western wall.

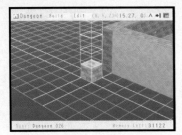

For the last two walls, we are going to employ a texturing shortcut. With your cursor still at coordinates 15,25,0, press and hold [R2]. Make sure Texture #98 is selected. While still holding [R2], press both [L2] and the left analog stick [L3]. This pastes the selected texture on all sides of the cube. If you move the cursor away from the wall, you can see the cube is now fully covered by the texture.

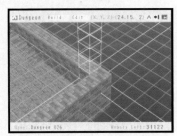

Texture the final two walls, and notice that unlike the first two walls, all the sides are fully covered by the selected texture. Go over the first two walls again to fully cover them.

Now let's apply a texture to the floor. Move the cursor to coordinates 24,16,0, and press and hold [R2]. Highlight Texture #111 and without releasing [R2], press both [L2] and the left analog stick [L3]. Release the buttons and the texture is pasted to all sides of the cursor cube. Tap ✕ and move

the cursor to the opposite corner of the room (coordinates 16,24,0). Tap ✕ and the floor is covered in the new texture.

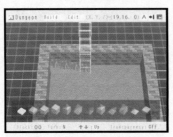

Feel free to texture the stairs as you choose. Placing textures is the same as placing blocks—be sure to select the correct size block for the stair you wish to texture (if you don't, the new block replaces the old one). For example, to texture the smallest stair, move the cursor so that it covers the stair (coordinates 19,16,1). Now, tap ▲ and highlight the first block from the left. Release ▲, then select your texture by pressing and holding [R2].

NOTE

Texturing already-created pieces illustrates one of the disadvantages of texturing without being in Texture mode—you are basically re-creating the piece from scratch, and, unless you're careful, you may alter more than just the texture. For this reason, it is wise to use this method from the beginning.

COPYING, PASTING, AND DELETING

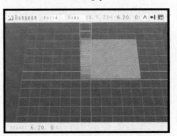

Create a small floor outside of the room you just textured and practice copying and pasting it, as well as deleting pieces from it.

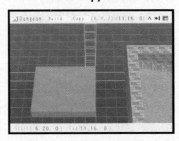

Enter Copy mode by pressing ■ + directional pad left. The cursor and grid turn blue, indicating you are in Copy mode.

Now, tap ✕ at one of the corners. Move to the opposite corner and tap ✕ again.

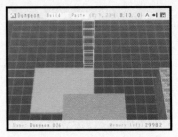

The cursor and grid automatically turn green to indicate you have entered Paste mode. Move the cursor outside your floor, and you notice it is dragging the copied portion. Tap ✕ to place the copied portion wherever you like.

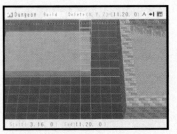

To delete the entire floor, press ■ + the directional pad down. The cursor and grid turn red to indicate that you have entered Delete mode. Now, move the cursor to one corner and tap ✕. Move the cursor to the opposite corner and tap ✕ again. The floor disappears.

NOTE

You can also copy, paste, and delete single blocks. Simply highlight the desired block and tap ✕ twice.

ADVANCED EDITING TECHNIQUES

Upon entering the Dungeon Editor screen, select the "Custom" tab to access several advanced options. We give you a quick overview of these options and leave you to use them in your own way.

Select the "Details" sub-menu and you have the option of changing the way blocks appear, altering the dungeon's background color, creating fog, and specifying the "Battle Screen."

BLOCK TRANSPARENCY

You can change the transparency of blocks by adjusting the transparency percentage. Use this feature if you want to create an invisible maze or simulate blocks of ice.

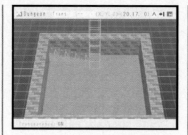

To place transparent blocks, enter the editor by selecting the "Edit" button. Enter Transparency mode by pressing ■ + L2. Now, turn on Transparency by pressing ▲ + the directional pad down.

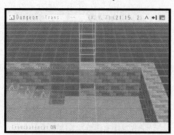

Now that Transparency mode is on, you can select already placed blocks and make them transparent. However, you cannot place new transparent blocks in Transparency mode. To place transparent blocks, press ■ + directional pad up to switch to Build/Edit mode. The blocks you place are now transparent. Remember to turn off Transparency by entering Transparency mode and pressing ▲ + directional pad up.

BLOCK DISTORTION

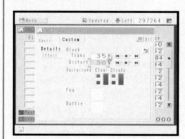

Change the amount of block distortion by raising and lowering the percentage.

Blocks do not show their distortion in Build/ Edit mode. You must enter View mode to see the effects of the distortion. To enter View mode, press ■ + R1.

TIP

The distortion feature is useful for creating a cavernlike dungeon. To achieve this effect, choose oddly shaped blocks to place, rather than the standard cube-shaped versions.

BACKGROUND AND FOG

Selecting a new background changes the color of the screen during editing and play.

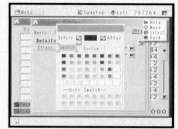

Selecting a color in the "Clear" field affects the background at all times, regardless of whether or not you have added clouds to your dungeon.

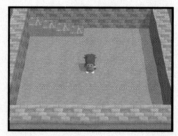

Changing the "Cloudy" color only affects the map if you change the "Clouds%" amount within the editor. To do so, enter the editor by selecting the "Edit" button. Switch to Confirm mode by pressing ■ + R2. Remember, this is just for viewing purposes. Weather and time of day effects are not set in the editor. If you want to set effects to the map, you must use script commands.

Now, press R1 + R2 to bring up the time and weather box. While holding R1 + R2, press L1. Now you can change the "Clouds%" by moving the directional pad left and right. The higher the percentage, the more the "Cloudy" color you selected appears.

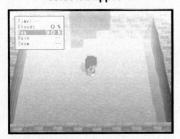

To switch to "Fog," press R1 + R2 + right analog button R3. The more you raise the percentage here, the more fog appears. You can change the fog color on the same page that you changed the background colors.

NOTE

Using different fog, clear, and cloudy colors allows for unlimited color schemes in your dungeon. Green fog can imply poison gas, while a darker color might resemble a smoke-filled room. Play around with all three to create any style you wish.

BATTLE

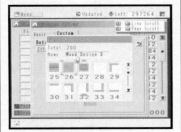

Change the "Battle" texture to specify the look of the ground when you enter a battle.

LIGHT AND SHADOW

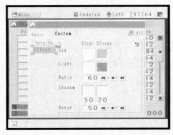

The "Effect" tab includes settings for "Sun" and "Shadow" effects.

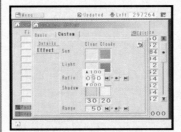

Up the "Ratio" to allow more light to bleed into your dungeon. If you set the value to zero, only environmental light is displayed.

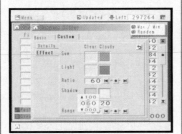

Darker shadows are created by increasing the values underneath the "Shadow" boxes; increasing the "Range" increases the length of the shadows.

TIP

You can create incredible atmospheric lighting by tweaking the sun and shadow settings. Add triangular blocks to the top of your dungeon walls, then choose yellow for the sun color and orange for the light color. Increase the shadow density and range, then enter the editor. Now, press and hold R1 + R2 to change the angle of the sun. You should get a spectacular lighting effect and a good idea of how to best use these advanced settings.

CREATING A BUILDING FROM SCRATCH

Buildings are basically objects, which then need only to be placed on a map. We don't need to create an interior, which is done within the Dungeon Editor. After we create a building—a house, for example—we can place a warp event at the entrance and link it to the dungeon we just created. We might then texture our dungeon to resemble the interior of the house. For our purposes, we use the Building Editor to construct the outside of the structure only.

Enter the Building database by selecting "Graphics," then "Building Editor" from the main menu. Select the "Create New Data" button and you enter the Building Editor screen. Select the "Basic" tab and enter a name for your creation. Exit the Text Input screen and select the "Edit" button to begin building a house.

BUILDING THE WALLS

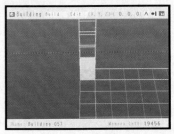

Does this screen look familiar? It uses the same interface and controls as the Dungeon Editor. We are going to assume that you understand the basics of building and texturing and are ready to do both jobs simultaneously. This makes the creation process much more efficient, once you get the hang of it.

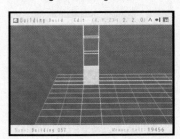

Move the cursor to coordinates 2,2,0. Pan the camera down by holding R1 and tapping up on the directional pad. Stop the camera when it is pointing at the front of the brick.

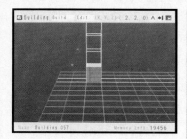

Press and hold [R2] to bring up the texture menu. Move the blinking texture selection box to "Texture: 17" and release [R2].

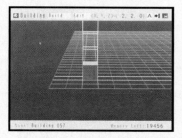

Rotate the camera until it faces the west side of the block. Press and hold [R2] and highlight "Texture: 18." Release [R2] and two sides of the cube are now textured.

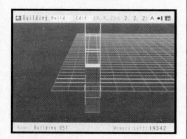

Tap X and press [L1] twice to move the cursor to coordinates 2,2,2. Tap X again and the corner of your house is built and textured.

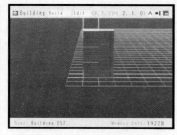

Move the cursor to the left one space to coordinates 2,1,2 and press and hold [R2]. Highlight "Texture: 16" and release [R2]. Tap X, then press [L2] twice to bring the blocks back to ground level. Tap X to set the wall.

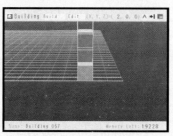

Move the cursor to coordinates 2,0,0 and press and hold [R2]. Highlight "Texture: 17" and release [R2]. Rotate the camera by holding [R1] and tapping the directional pad to the left two times.

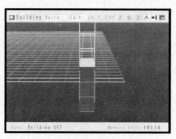

Hold [R2], highlight "Texture: 18," and release [R2]. Tap X, then tap [L1] twice, and tap X once again. This creates the second corner of our beautiful house.

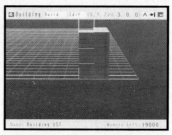

You should be getting the hang of this by now. Create the next part of the house by selecting "Texture: 16" and placing the three blocks from coordinates 3,0,2 to coordinates 3,0,0.

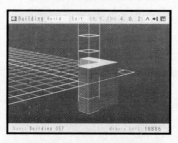

For the third corner, select "Texture: 17" for the side the camera is facing, and "Texture: 18" for the east side (you have to rotate the camera). Place the blocks from coordinates 4,0,0 to coordinates 4,0,2.

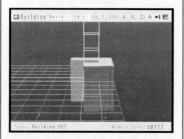

The middle part of the third side consists of "Texture: 16."

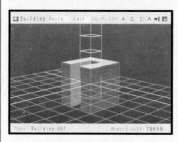

The last corner will include "Texture: 17" for the side the camera is facing and "Texture: 18" for the front side.

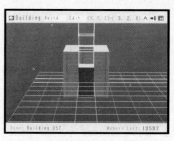

To create the door (or opening to be more precise), move the cursor to coordinates 3,2,0 and select "Texture: 0" (a blank texture). Tap X, press [L1] once, then tap X again.

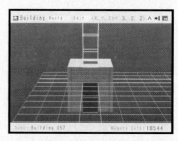

Finally, move the cursor to coordinates 3,2,2 and highlight "Texture: 16" to finish the foundation.

NOTE

Because the party won't actually enter the structure we are building, the interior can be solid.

BUILDING THE ROOF

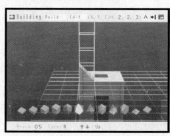

Move the cursor to coordinates 2,2,3 and press and hold ▲. The block selection screen should pop up. Move the directional pad right until "Block: 05" is highlighted (it's the sixth block from the left).

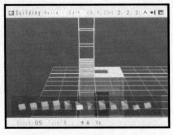

Still pressing ▲, rotate the left analog stick clockwise until the block rotates once toward you. Its slope is now facing the camera.

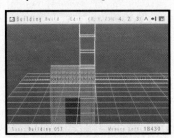

Release ▲, then press R2 to select "Texture: 74." Now, still holding R2, press L2 + left analog button L3 to set the texture on all sides of the block. Tap X to set the starting point for your roof, then move the cursor right two spaces to coordinates 4,2,3. Tap X to set the blocks.

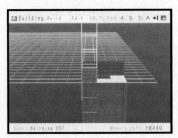

Move the cursor to coordinates 4,0,3 and rotate the camera until it faces the back of the house. To rotate the camera, press and hold R1 and tap the directional pad right or left.

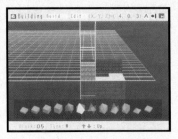

We need to create a sloped roof on this side as well, but the block is facing the wrong way. To rotate the block, press and hold ▲, then rotate the left analog stick clockwise until the slope of the block is facing you. Release ▲ and tap X to set the block's starting point. Move the cursor to coordinates 2,0,3, and tap X once more to set the roof.

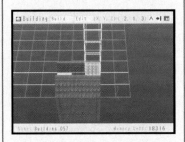

We need to fill in the center of the roof with blocks. Move the cursor to coordinates 2,1,3, then press and hold ▲ and select "Block: 03." Release ▲ and pan the camera up so we are looking down on the roof (hold R1 and press the directional pad down).

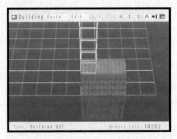

Press and hold R2 and highlight "Texture: 16." Release R2 and place the blocks to the other side of the roof (to coordinates 4,1,3).

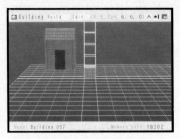

That's it, your first house! It may be small, but remember: because the interior is built elsewhere, it can be as large as you wish.

NOTE

Now that you have the basics down, alter and expand the house to suit your vision. Remember that copying and pasting is a fast way to double the size of a building.

OBJECT PLACEMENT

A while back we created a dungeon. Now let's decorate it. To do so, select "Graphics," then "Object Placement" from the main menu. The Object Placement database pops up. We want to create a brand new Object Set for our dungeon, so select "Create New Data." Change the generic Object Set name to something more befitting your creation, then move the cursor into the "Data: Dungeon Database" bubble and select it. Now, highlight "-None-" and tap X. Scroll up and select the dungeon you created earlier. Finally, select the "Edit" button to begin placing objects in your dungeon.

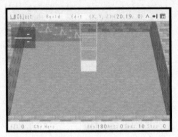

Remember this place? it's a bit dreary, even as dungeons go, so let's add a few knickknacks to liven it up.

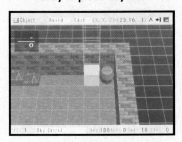

Move the cursor up against the northern corner to coordinates 24,16,1. Tap X and a blinking character appears. As we aren't interested in dropping in a character, tap ■ to switch to object placement. A blinking barrel appears, signaling you're ready to place objects.

Tap X again and the barrel is placed.

TIP

Keep the Object Appendix located in the back of this guide handy when placing items, because there are more than 250 objects to browse through.

Let's place a carpet in the middle of the room. Looking at the Object list in the back of the guide, we can see that Object #159 looks good. To scroll through the objects individually, tap right or left on the directional pad. To scroll through every tenth item, press up or down on the directional pad. Tap X once you find the blue carpet.

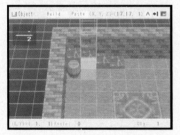

It's that simple. Browse through the various objects and practice placing them as you see fit. To delete a placed item, press ■ + down on the control pad. To copy an item, press ■ + left on the directional pad.

You can also place buildings on the world map you created. Simply enter the Object Placement database ("Graphics," "Object Placement" from the main menu) and select "Create New Data." Name your Object Set and pull up your created world within the "Data/Map Database" field.

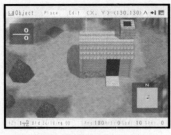

Select the "Edit" button and move the pointer to where you'd like a building placed. Now, tap X, then ■ twice to enter Building Placement. Scroll through the buildings and place the one you like with a tap of the X button.

NOTE

An important message about the difference between Objects and Events: Objects are items, characters, or buildings that you in no way interact with. They are simply decorations. If you want to talk to them, examine them, or interact with them in any way, they need to be created as events, not objects.

For example, placing a treasure chest in your dungeon is fine, but if you want that chest to open and yield treasure, you must create an event for it, then place it in Event Placement. See the next chapter to learn more about events.

OBJECT MODELS

You may wish to create your own objects, or at least alter the existing ones. To do so, select "Graphics," then "Object Models" from the main menu. Select "Create New Data" and the Object Editor pops up.

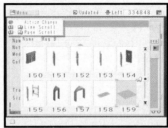

Highlight the "Model" field and tap X. Now pick a model to alter. Let's select that blue carpet again. It's called "Rug B" and its number is 159.

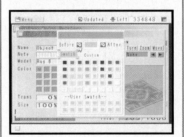

Tap X once the rug is highlighted, and you return to the editor. Select the "Color" field by pressing X over the gray box. The entire carpet starts blinking, letting you know that picking a new color will alter the color of the entire carpet.

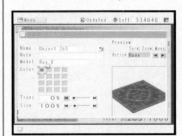

Pick a color that suits you and select it within the "Swatch" menu.

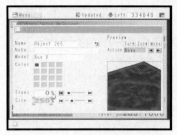

If you want to change the carpet's size, highlight the "Size" field and change the value. You can create a rug of almost any size, perfect if a snooty noble needs wall-to-wall carpeting.

Name the item you have altered and exit the database, remembering to update your data. Your custom object is now available in the Object Placement Editor.

WORLD ORGANIZATION

World Organization is a necessary step to link the pieces of our creation together. Enter "World Organization" by selecting "Graphics," then "World Organization" from the main menu.

The World Organization database contains all the pre-existing areas in the game. We need to add our maps to it. Select "Create New Data" to do so.

Select the "Basic Tab" and highlight the "Name" field. Notice the generic name says "World Set." The whole point of this screen is to link all our created objects, events, units, music, and sound effects to a particular map or dungeon. The completed puzzle is called a World Set.

NOTE

Even though you may have placed objects on the map earlier, they are not activated until you link them to the map here. The same goes for events, units, music, and sound effects, but we talk about those later.

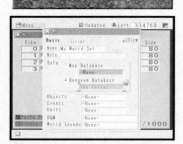

We are going to link the Object Set you placed in your dungeon earlier to the dungeon itself. Tap ✕ to bring up the Text Input screen and choose a name for the Dungeon Set. Next, move the cursor down to the "Data" box and select the bubble next to "Dungeon Database." Finally, highlight "-None-" and choose the dungeon you created from the list that pops up.

Now we have to select everything that we want to appear and occur within the dungeon's confines. Select the "Objects" field, then select the Object Set we created earlier.

Thus far we have only created an Object Set for our dungeon, so we are done for now. To see how your decorated dungeon looks, select the "View" button to the right of the "Script" tab.

NOTE

Once you create an Event Set, a Unit Set, a Background Music Set, and a World Sounds Set for your dungeon, return to the World Organization database, select the dungeon's World Set, select "Edit," then call them up just as you did the Objects Set.

We also created a World Map earlier. We have to create a World Set for it as well. Return to the World Organization database by pressing ● twice, remembering to update your data. Select "Create New Data."

Input a name for your World Set, then move the cursor down to the "Data/Map Database" field. Select "-None-" and select your World Map from the Map database. If you created an Object Set for the map, select it within the "Objects" field.

NOTE

You need to create a World Set for every map, dungeon, or interior you create.

SCRIPT AND EVENT CREATION

SCRIPTS

Events make the world go 'round, and scripts make up events. Whether you want to set up a conversation with a villager, do battle with a monster, or open a treasure box, you need to put together a script, then specify it as the event you want. Got it? Don't worry—it all becomes clear as we go through it. Enter the Script database by selecting "Scripts" and then "Scripts" again from the main menu.

The Script database contains just under 400 pre-existing scripts. Spend some time looking through these scripts to see how certain operations are performed.

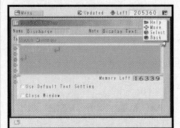

Select "Create New Data" to enter the Script Editor. You can change the name of the script and select the script type as well. Highlight the large white box and press ✕ to access the Script Creation menu.

NOTE

Choose from four types of scripts. "Page Condition" sets detailed conditions that must be met before an event occurs. "Action" scripts are called out in the "Motion" field of the Event Editor. "Start Condition" scripts allow you to control in detail what starts an event. All other scripts are "Content" scripts. When we get into the Event Editor, we'll talk more about the script types.

NOTE

One of the pre-existing scripts within the Script Database contains an error that causes multiple abilities to execute incorrectly. To fix this, enter the Scripts Database and select File number 88, "Discharge." Select "Edit," then highlight Script Command line 02. Select "Edit" and remove both the question mark and one of the two return symbols. Update your data and the script will be fixed!

PARTY

The first menu option deals with the party as a whole. You find, for example, commands to increase the party's gold, add items to their bag, or teleport them to different places.

POSSESSIONS

The Possessions sub-menu allows you to tweak the party's possessions, including gold and items.

MONEY: Use this Script Command anytime you want to add to, subtract from, or overwrite the amount of gold in the party's possession. For example, if the party is robbed, you may subtract 50g from its bag.

ITEM: Use this to add, subtract, or overwrite the items that the party has in its bag. For example, a villager may give the party an item after a quest is completed, or a pickpocket might take a certain item away.

EMPTY BAG: This removes all items from the party's bag. You might use this script when the party completes the first act in your game and you want them to begin the next act with nothing.

USE BAG: This command allows the bag to be used. If you already enabled bag usage in "Game/General Settings/Custom/Bag," you won't need this command. Use it only if you started the party out without the bag and at some point in the game want them to be able to use it.

MEMBERS

This allows you to alter the member structure within your party.

FORMATION: This option allows you to change the formation of the party.

CHANGE: This option allows you to add or remove party members. Note that when you remove a member, they take their items with them unless you specified "Can Not Discard" within the Item Editor. Make sure you set crucial quest items to "Can Not Discard" before you remove a member. Also, enable bag usage so you have access to those important items.

LEADER: Allows you to change the party's leader. Story-conscious creators can change leaders if, for example, the current leader lets the party down or an upstart character overtakes the current leader.

MOVEMENT

These are commands that deal with the party's movement.

DIRECTION MOVE: This allows you to move the party a specified direction, at a specified speed, to a specified location. Use this command to point the party in the right direction.

LOCATION MOVE: This moves the party to a specified location on a map at a specified speed. Use this to condense time and get the party to its destination more quickly.

DIRECTION CHANGE: This allows you to turn the leader,

or the whole party, to face a specified direction. You can also set the time it takes to make the turn. One frame equals 1/30th of a second. If you set the frame rate low, they turn to face an enemy in slow motion.

ROTATE: This command allows you to rotate the leader or the entire party at a specified angle and to dictate how much time it takes for the rotation to occur.

VERTICAL MOVE: Move the leader or the party to a specified height with this command. While in motion, they pass through all objects, land masses, and buildings.

LANDING: Use this to lower a designated member or the leader to the ground in a designated time frame. This is useful when landing a flying vehicle.

GATHER: This places all of the party members on top of the leader. Use this command when you want it to appear that the party is entering a vehicle.

BYPASS OBJECTS: This Script Command allows the party to bypass all objects or allows them to enter an object.

DISPLAY

This command changes how the party is displayed. Hide all members, or just show the leader. This is useful when the party is on a boat or other vehicle. If you would prefer to show only the leader traversing a map, use this command.

FLOAT

This command moves the party vertically to a specified height. Members float there until you use this command again to move them back down. While floating, they cannot pass through objects.

TELEPORT

The Teleport commands allow you to instantly move your party to a specified point.

WARP: Use this to warp your party from a World Map to a dungeon, a Town Map to an interior, a downstairs room to an upstairs room, and so on. See "Quick Start" for a detailed example.

WARP TO SAVED: Use this to move the party to their last save point. If the party is defeated in battle, insert this command so the group can restart nearby.

TELEPORT: Use this command to allow the party to teleport to locations set within the Set Teleport command.

SET TELEPORT: This command allows you to set a specified teleport location, or to automatically set a location

for teleport once a party reaches it. Use this as a bind point for your party.

DELETE TELEPORT: Allows you to delete a specified teleport point.

ESCAPE: Allows the party to escape to a specified escape location.

SET ESCAPE: Set an escape point for your party here (at the entrance to a dungeon, for example).

DELETE ESCAPE: Deletes a specified escape location.

MEMBERS

The Members menu contains Script Commands related to individual members. Any member listed in the Party Member database can be affected by these commands.

NOTE

All these commands (except the "Member/Effects" command) work whether or not the member is currently in your party.

ATTRIBUTES

This command allows you to alter the attributes of party members. You can change 11 attributes. You can add, subtract, or overwrite any party member's current attribute value with a new value of your choice.

NOTE

You cannot set a value for hit points and magic points that exceed the values set within "Max HP" and "Max MP," respectively. First raise the attribute limits, then raise the attributes.

BASIC INFO

This command allows you to alter basic member information such as name, level, and rank.

NAME: Specify a new name for a character or select an input variable that contains the new name. Should you wish to give the player the option to enter a name, use this Script Command in conjunction with the Input Creation/Text Script Command.

ORIGIN: Like the Name command, this option allows you to specify the origin of a character or let the current content of an input variable determine the change.

BIO: This allows you to delete or add to the biography of a character, updating a party member's bio as more information is learned about him.

SEX: This allows you to change a member's sex or make other differentiations (you can make "Sex" mean gender, tribe, race, or whatever). You can name the generic sex entries within "Game/Game Settings/Custom/Sex."

WEAPON PROPERTY: This allows you to change the unarmed weapon property of a specific member. For example, attacks may be set to "Slash" at a certain level. This could be good or bad depending on how many creatures have resistance to or are vulnerable to slash damage.

EXPERIENCE: Allows you to add, subtract, or overwrite experience points for a certain member. You may gain experience for finishing a quest, or lose experience for handling a task contrary to a character's alignment.

LEVEL: You can add or subtract a specified number of levels for a character or specify a level for that character.

CLASS: Allows you to change the class of a character.

CLASS RANK: Allows you to add or subtract a specified number of ranks to a character's class.

CLASS EXPERIENCE: Allows you to add experience to a specified member's class.

BATTLE VICTORY: Allows you to add or subtract a number of battle victories to a member.

ITEM: This allows you to add or remove an item from a member's inventory. You cannot add to an already full inventory.

NOTE

As with experience, a succession of battle victories usually leads to an increase in level. To learn how adding experience or victories affects the character's rank and title, see "Game/ Classes/ Custom/ Promote."

EQUIP AND ABILITIES

This menu allows you to alter the equipment of members and grant them new abilities.

EQUIPMENT SETTINGS: This command allows you to specify whether or not a member can unequip weapons, helmets, armor, shields, or accessories. A spell may cause this, or a demonic sword that once equipped cannot be removed.

Should you want to grant the member the ability to unequip that item at any time, use the "Members/Basic Info/Item" or "Members/Equip and Abilities/Remove Equipment" Script Commands.

EQUIP: Allows you to make a member equip a designated item that he or she has in inventory.

REMOVE EQUIPMENT: Allows the member to remove a designated type of item. Use this even if you have used an Equipment Settings Script Command to specify that the same type of item cannot be removed.

ABILITY: This allows you to grant or remove an ability from a particular member.

STATUS

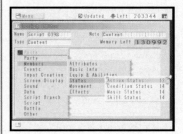

This menu allows you to manage member statuses.

ACTION STATUS: This allows you to apply or remove an abnormal status to a character. Abnormal action statuses prevent the character from performing any actions. "Blind," "Sleep," and "Numb" are examples of action statuses. Confirm an action status here to determine other events. For example, you can confirm the death status. If it's true, you can revive that character.

CONDITION STATUS: Condition statuses are any effects that raise or lower attributes. "Poison" and "Decrease Armor" are examples of condition statuses. You can confirm a condition status here. For example, if agility is somehow increased, you can bestow on that character an ability it wouldn't otherwise have.

MAGIC STATUS: Any status that prevents a member from casting spells is an abnormal magic status. "Silence" is an example of a magic status.

SKILL STATUS: Any status that disallows the use of skills is a skill status. "Seal" is the only pre-existing type of skill status.

MOVEMENT

This menu allows you to manage the movement of individual party members.

NOTE

See the descriptions under "Party/ Movement" for the majority of these commands. Only those commands unique to "Member/ Movement" are discussed below.

BYPASS MEMBERS: Enabling bypass by selecting "Yes" allows other characters to move right through the specified member.

LAY DOWN: This allows you to change the member's position relative to the ground, to a specified height in a specified amount of time.

EFFECTS

This menu allows you to temporarily change member effects such as color, model, and transparency.

DISPLAY: Toggles the appearance of the member's model on and off. Even though the model may be invisible, it is still present. Collisions still occur as usual.

MODEL: Allows you to change the model of a party member.

TRANSPARENCY: Set the transparency for a particular member with this command. "0" equals completely visible and "100" equals completely transparent. You can also set the time it takes for the character to reach the specified transparency.

COLOR: Allows you to change the color of a character model. Change the color of various pieces of the model as you would in Model Editor. You can create a blush or a sickly look by changing a model's face to an appropriate color.

SIZE: This allows you to change the size of a member. Make him appear fattened after a large meal, or taller throughout the course of the adventure.

FLASH: Allows the character model to disappear and reappear at specified

intervals. There are 30 frames in a second, so if you want the model to appear for 10 seconds and disappear for 5, enter "300" in the Show field and "150" in the Hide field.

MOTION CHANGE: Change the normal motion of the model here. Many models have special actions that can be used with this Script Command. If you want the action to be used only once, use the Single Action Script Command.

SINGLE ACTION: The same as the Motion Change command but you get the option to "Disable Motion After Action." Use this if you want a model to express happiness just once, then resume their usual action.

LOOK: This command allows you to permanently change the facial expression of a character. Use the same Script Command to revert to the normal facial expression.

SHADOW: Toggles a member's shadow on and off.

DEFAULT: Returns the character model to the default settings. Any changes you made in transparency, color, and size revert to default.

EVENTS

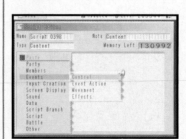

The following Script Commands relate to the performance of events.

CONTROL

This menu contains Script Commands relating to the starting and management of Events.

START: This command enables you to allow or disallow the start of an event.

TEMPORARY REMOVAL: This command allows you to delete the event temporarily.

DUPLICATE: This allows you to duplicate a single event or even multiple events to a specific point on a map. The duplicate event disappears when a character returns to the same location.

CHANGE: This command allows you to apply script commands to another event within this event's script. An example would be if you were talking to a character and when that character says something you could have another event walk up to you and listen. Normally, if you wanted an event to walk up to you the commands would have to be within that other event's script. Basically it allows you to control another event while still in the current event's script.

EVENT INFO LOAD: Loads the current Event's info into the appropriate flags and variables. Specifically, it loads:

Variable 067: Event: X Coordinate

Variable 068: Event: Y Coordinate

Variable 069: Event: Z Coordinate

Variable 070: Event: Direction

Variable 071: Event: Number

Input Variable 005: Event

Flag 050: Event Condition

EVENT INFO SAVE: Saves the current Event's information into the appropriate flags and variable. Specifically, it saves:

Variable 071: Event: Number

Input Variable 005: Event

Flag 050: Event Condition

For the Event Info Load and Save commands, the variables and flags that are loaded/saved are only used within a map. If you warp, it goes back to its default setting.

EVENT ACTION

The following Script Commands dictate the movement and actions of non-party members. This menu is not available unless the script "Type" is set to "Action."

RANDOM: Create a character that moves in random directions for a specified number of steps.

EAST/WEST: Create a character that moves east to west and back again. If the character bumps into something, it turns around and walks the other way.

NORTH/SOUTH: Create a character that moves north to south and back again. If the character bumps into something, it turns around and walks the other way.

TO LEADER: The event moves to the leader of the party, as long as nothing blocks its way.

TO PARTY: An event follows behind the party. For example, a dog might follow the party until the leader gives it an item.

ACT AS MEMBER: This command makes an event act like a member of the party. It walks with the party and even rides with them in a vehicle, but it does not fight with them.

LEAVE LEADER: This makes an event move away from the leader. A guilty or scared villager may act this way.

UP AND DOWN: Set the event to move continuously up and down.

MOVEMENT

This menu deals with the movement of events on a map. Refer to the "Party/Movement" and "Members/Movement" sections above for more details.

EFFECTS

This menu allows you to change the appearance of events. See the "Members/Effects" section above for more information.

INPUT CREATION

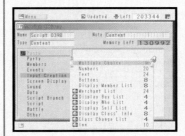

The Input Creation menu deals with events that allow the player to input text or numbers, or to choose an answer from a multiple choice question.

MULTIPLE CHOICE: This command allows you to pose a multiple-choice question to the party. See "Quick Start" for an example of how to create a multiple-choice event.

NUMBERS: This command creates a window into which the player can enter a number. You can set the numerical boundaries of the choice as well. Create, for example, an event such as "Pick a Number Between 1 and 10," in which the party earns rewards or suffers penalties depending on its choice.

TEXT: Allows the player to enter text. Most commonly, the player names his or her character.

BUTTONS: This command prompts the user to press a button before the event continues.

DISPLAY MEMBER LIST: This command creates a window with the party members' names listed, allowing the player to choose a member.

MERCHANT LIST: Select up to seven items that can be purchased from a merchant. Select the script you set up within "Display Buy List" in the Merchant Script field.

DISPLAY BUY LIST: This displays the item list that you set up in Merchant List.

DISPLAY WHO LIST: Allows the player to choose to whom the purchased item is given.

DISPLAY SELL LIST: Displays a list of the party's inventory so the player can choose which items to sell.

DISPLAY CLASS INFO: This displays information on the classes.

CLASS CHANGE LIST: Displays a window that allows the player to choose a new class.

INN: This displays the Inn window, so you can set up an inn.

SCREEN DISPLAY

This menu deals with what is displayed onscreen. From text to camera angles, you can determine how certain events are displayed.

TEXT

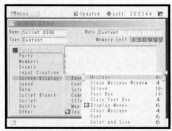

This sub-menu deals with the appearance of onscreen text.

MESSAGE: This allows you to enter text that appears within a message box. This command is used for displaying conversations.

CLOSE MESSAGE WINDOW: Closes whatever message window is open.

SCREEN: This command allows you to enter text that is not displayed within a message box. You can specify whether the text you enter appears as fixed text, or rolls up like movie credits.

TEXT BOX: This allows you to enter text within a text box of a specified size and at a specified location. Any message boxes that were created in Message appear behind the text entered here. Use the Close Text Box command to close the box.

CLOSE TEXT BOX: Removes the display created with the Text Box command.

DISPLAY MONEY: This command allows you to toggle the party's money display on and off. If it's toggled on, the money display appears in the upper right corner of the screen.

CLEAR MESSAGE: Clear the text that you entered in Message. It doesn't work with text created using the Text Box command.

FONT: Change the look of all the text in the game.

COLOR AND SIZE: Change the color and size of the text you enter using the Message command.

CONTENT

The contents of menu text, variables, and inputs are displayed using this menu.

VARIABLE: Allows you to display the contents of a variable as part of a message.

INPUT: Allows you to display the contents of an input variable as part of a message. If you are fuzzy on the usage of input variables, press START to read through the description in the Help menu.

MENU TEXT: Displays the specified menu text in the message window.

DESCRIPTION: This allows you to display a specified class, trait, item, or ability description in a message window.

NOTE

Using an input variable that contains the main character's name is necessary if you want an NPC to greet the player and if you allow the player to the main character's name.

SCREEN EFFECTS

This menu allows the creation of screen effects as well as time and weather effects.

MASK: This creates a frame of a designated color and designated size around the screen.

COLOR: This applies a color to the screen. You can specify the color, the color's transparency, and the time it takes for it to occur.

SHAKE: This command shakes the screen. Use this to simulate explosions, earthquakes, or the party being hit.

LINGER: This command makes a previous screen linger on top of the current screen. The lingering screen can be set to a specific transparency.

WEATHER: Use this command to change the weather to rain, snow, fog, or clouds. You can also specify the strength of the weather and the time it takes to achieve the change.

TIME: This command changes the time of day to dawn, noon, dusk, or night. The lighting changes accordingly.

DEFAULT: The effects set with the Shake, Color, Linger, Mask, or Weather commands revert to the default settings.

CAMERA

This menu allows you to customize the camera settings.

ROTATE: Rotate the camera in a specified direction at a specified rate.

CUSTOM ROTATE: Prohibits the player from fully controlling camera rotation.

DISTANCE: Zoom the camera in and out a specified distance at a specified rate.

VIEWPOINT ANGLE: Alter the angle of the camera vertically.

HORIZONTAL ANGLE: Change the horizontal angle of the camera.

HEIGHT: Change the camera to a specified height at a specified rate.

VIEWPOINT HEIGHT: Change the viewpoint (the point at which the camera is pointing) height of the camera. The angle remains the same.

VIEWPOINT TARGET: For use in battle only, this command changes the viewpoint of the camera to the target of attack.

DEFAULT: All changes made to the camera, except those made in Rotate and Custom Rotate, revert to default settings.

EFFECTS

These commands deal with effects created within the Visual Effects Editor.

LOCATION: Apply your created effect at a specified location on a specified map. Also, set how many times your effect occurs. Use this to place a lightning strike event or an explosion.

PARTY: This makes your visual effect target either the party leader or the entire party.

MEMBER: Specify an individual member as the target for a visual effect.

EVENT: Display the effect on a designated event.

TARGET: Apply the effect to an enemy in battle. Call this Script up within "Direct Effect/Custom/Directing" in either the Success, Critical, Custom, or Fail field. For example, a lighting effect could designate a successful critical hit on an enemy.

VIEWPOINT: Set the effect to occur at the viewpoint of the camera while in battle.

SET WIPE: Sets up the wipe transition that you specify in Apply Wipe. Wipe refers to the transition of the screen when you enter a battle.

APPLY WIPE: Applies the wipe that you set up in Set Wipe. If you don't "Set Wipe", the wipe called for in "Game/General Settings/Custom/Battle/Screen Effects" is used.

IMAGE: Load a digital camera image or a screenshot into memory for quick usage later.

CLEAR ALL EFFECTS: Clear all the effects present on the map.

MAP

These commands relate to the display of the World Map.

DISPLAY MAP: Show the World Map at a specified location on the screen for a specified amount of time. Also, choose markers for the party and other objects.

REMOVE MAP: Remove the map that is currently displayed.

SEA LEVEL

This command raises or lowers the sea level to a specified height. It only changes the appearance, so if you flooded a city with this command, your party could still wade through the water.

SOUND

This menu contains Script Commands related to sound.

BGM: Changes the background music to a specified tune with a specified volume, pitch, and tempo.

WORLD SOUNDS: Specify a sound such as crickets or thunder to begin playing at a specified volume, pitch, and tempo.

SFX: Play a sound effect at a specified volume, pitch, and tempo. Also, make the effect play through the right speaker, the left speaker, or both. Sound effects stop after they play once.

SOUND CONTROL: Use this command to fade into or out of a background music selection.

STOP: Instantly stop all background music, world sounds, and SFX.

TEMPORARY SAVE: Temporarily save a map's BGM and world sounds. Use Replay Saved to replay the saved sounds. This is especially useful if you want the BGM and sounds to resume after the party finishes a battle.

REPLAY SAVED: Begins playing any sound files that were saved using the Temporary Save command.

BATTLE MUSIC: This plays the background music and world sounds designated in "Game/General Setting/Custom/Battle."

MAP MUSIC: Plays the background music and world sounds that were set up in "Graphics/World Organization/Basic."

DATA

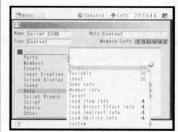

This menu allows you to compose Script Commands that deal with data handling such as variables and with calling up group and game information.

FLAGS

This allows you to change the status of a specified flag. For example, acquiring a specific item could switch on a specified flag. Then you could create an event that would occur only if that flag were on. If you want that event to occur only once, you would include this Script Command again, but this time to switch the flag off.

VARIABLE

You can modify the contents of a specified variable here. For example, you can choose a random number between 1 and 100, or you can add, subtract, multiply, or divide two variables or set numbers.

INPUT

This Script Command allows you to change the contents of one input variable to the contents of another input variable or specified line of text.

GAME INFO

Selecting "Load" loads many game settings into their appropriate flags, variables, and input variables. Then you can access and manipulate them as desired. If you enter a number in *Variable 134: Item Number*, this command will return

quantity info on the selected item. Below is a list of what is loaded, and where:

Variable 075:Party Member Total

Variable 077:Total Party Money

Variable 081:Map Number

Variable 082:Party:X Coordinate

Variable 083:Party:Y Coordinate

Variable 084:Party:Z Coordinate

Variable 085:Party:Direction

Variable 079:Total Bag Items

Variable 078:Total Party Items

Variable 80:Total Items (Quantity of the designated item in the bag)

Flag 032:Escape Set is on if escape location is registered.

Flag 033:Teleport Set is on if there is at least one teleport location.

Selecting "Save" updates *Variable 077:Total Party Money.*

MEMBER INFO

USE MEMBER ORDER:

Acquire a party member's database number from that member's order in the party by putting their order number into *Variable 053:Member Order.* The database number of the member is entered into *Variable 086:Member Number* and *Variable 048:Instigator Number.*

LOAD: If you use this command after inputting the member's database number in *Variable 086:Member Number,* all information related to that member is loaded, including:

Variable 099:Strength

Variable 100:Defend

Variable 101:Intelligence

Variable 102:Agility

Variable 103:Luck

Variable 104:Attack

Variable 105:Armor

Variable 106:Max Hit Points

Variable 107:Max Magic Points

The above figures are corrected if *Flag 081:Stat Check Type* is on. If the flag is off, the figures are not corrected (except attack and armor). The status of *Flag 081:Stat Check Type* does not affect:

Variable 097:Hit Points

Variable 098:Magic Points

Variable 091:Level

Variable 095:Experience

Variable 092:Experience to Level

Input 001:Common Name

Input 006:Origin

Input 007:Sex

Other data loaded includes:

Variable 087:Total Member Items

Variable 117:Item (1) to *Variable 128:Item (12)* These include the Item database number of those items or "-1" if the member does not have an item.

Variable 129:Weapon Equipped to *Variable 133:Accessory Equipped* These include the Equipped Item database number.

Flag 140:Can't Remove Weapon to *Flag 144:Can't Remove Accessory* are on if the equipment at each location is set as "Can Not Remove."

Flag 121:Action Status is on if the member is under an abnormal action status.

Variable 088:Class Number reflects the database number of the character's current class.

Variable 090:Class Rank, Variable 112:Class Experience, Variable 113:Class Victories, Variable 093:Class Experience to Level, Variable 094:Victories to Level are loaded if the character is in a class.

Flag 040:Member Present is on if the member is in the party.

Variable 108:Target:X Coordinate, Variable 109:Target:Y Coordinate, Variable 110:Target:Z Coordinate, and *Variable 111:Target:Direction* are loaded if the character is in a party.

Flag 180–189 Normal Flag, Variable 180–189 Normal Variable, and *Input 018:Normal Input Variable* are affected if the character is not in a battle.

Flag 190–199 Battle Flag, Variable 190–199 Battle Variable, and *Input 019:Battle Input Variable* are affected if the character is in a battle.

SAVE: The member's current data are saved to the following flags and variables when you input the member's Party Member database number into *Variable 086:Member Number,* then select the "Data/Member Info/Save" Script Command:

Variable 099:Strength

Variable 100:Defend

Variable 101:Intelligence

Variable 102:Agility

Variable 103:Luck

Variable 104:Attack

Variable 105:Armor

Variable 106:Max Hit Points

Variable 107:Max Magic Points

The above figures are corrected if *Flag 081:Stat Check Type* is on. If the flag is off, the figures are not corrected (except attack and armor). The status of *Flag 081:Stat Check Type* does not affect:

Variable 097:Hit Points

Variable 098:Magic Points

Variable 091:Level

Variable 095:Experience

IF IN A CLASS: *Variable 090:Class Rank, Variable 112:Class Experience,* and *Variable 113:Class Victories* are loaded.

IF NOT IN A BATTLE: *Flag 180–189 Normal Flag, Variable 180–189 Normal Variable,* and *Input 018:Normal Input Variable* are affected.

IF IN A BATTLE: *Flag 190–199 Battle Flag, Variable 190–199 Battle Variable,* and *Input 019:Battle Input Variable* are affected.

TARGET

Target refers to the target of a Direct Effect. Both enemies and party members can be targets.

NOTE

Check the descriptions in the "Member Info" section for more detailed information. The only difference between the Member and the Target Script Command options is that the Target menu does not include the command options for movement and effects.

LOAD ITEM INFO

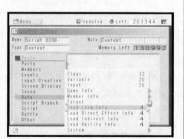

If you use *Variable 134:Item Number, Variable 085:Member Number,* and *Variable 088:Class Number* as inputs, then apply this command, the item's info is loaded into:

Variable 135:Item:Type

Variable 136:Item:Buy Price

Variable 137:Item:Sell Price

Variable 138:Item:Weapon Property

Variable 139:Used Direct Effect

Variable 140:Item:Type: Used Indirect Effect

Variable 141:Item: Equipped (HP)

Variable 142:Item: Equipped (MP)

Variable 143:Item: Equipped (STR)

Variable 144:Item: Equipped (DEF)

Variable 145:Item: Equipped (INT)

Variable 146:Item: Equipped (AGI)

Variable 147:Item: Equipped (LUCK)

Variable 151:Item:Attack Direct Effect

Variable 152:Item:Attack Indirect

And the following flags are switched appropriately:

Flag 130:Hide Item Info

Flag 131:Unsellable Item

Flag 132:Indestructible Item

Flag 133:Member Can't Equip Item

Flag 134:Member Can't Remove Item

Flag 135:Class Can't Equip Item

Flag 135:Class Can't R emove Item

Finally, *Input Variable 001:Common Name* is loaded.

LOAD DIRECT EFFECT INFO

If you use *Variable 163:Direct Effect Number* as the input, then apply this command, the Direct Effect's info loads into:

Variable 164:Direct:Rate

Variable 165:Direct: Success Ratio

Variable 166:Direct:Type

Variable 167:Direct: Target Type

Variable 168:Direct:Menu

Variable 169:Direct:Range

Flag 160:Direct Effect Death Check

Input 001:Common Name

LOAD INDIRECT INFO

You can load the specified Indirect Effect's information by using *Variable 172:Indirect Number* as the first input. You then need to enter the Indirect Effect's Property number into: *Variable 036:Instigator Magic Property* and *Variable 037:Instigator Weapon Property* to check for resistances. Now, apply this Script Command and the following information is loaded:

*Variable 173:Indirect:
Weapon Resist*

*Variable 174:Indirect: Magic
Resist*

Variable 175:Indirect: Priority

Variable 176:Indirect:Rate

Variable 177:Indirect:Type

Input 001:Common Name

LOAD ABILITY INFO

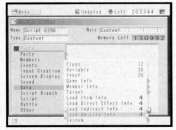

To load a designated
ability's info, enter the
ability's database number
into [Variable 155:Ability
Number], then apply this
Script Command. The
following info is loaded:

Variable 156:Ability:Cost

*Variable 157:Ability: Direct
Effect*

*Variable 158:Ability: Indirect
Effect*

Variable 159:Ability: Usable

*Variable 160:Ability: Random
Type*

Flag 150:Ability Type

Flag 151:Hide Ability Info

Input 001:Common Name

SYSTEM

The following Script
Commands relate to the
battle system.

SUBSTITUTE ATTRIBUTE FOR VARIABLE

This allows you to substitute
the applicable target's
attributes for the contents of
variables. Using the applicable target's information as
the input, the output looks
like this:

Variable 099:Strength

Variable 100:Defend

Variable 101:Intelligence

Variable 102:Agility

Variable 103:Luck

Variable 104:Attack

Variable 105:Armor

Variable 106:Max Hit Points

*Variable 107:Max Magic
Points*

The above figures are
corrected if [Flag 081:Stat
Check Type] is on. If the flag
is off, the figures are not
corrected (except Attack and
Armor). The status of [Flag
081:Stat Check Type] does
not affect:

Variable 097:Hit Points

Variable 098:Magic Points

Other data loaded include:

Variable 117:Item (1) to
Variable 128:Item (12)
includes the Item database
number of those items, or "-1"
if the member does not have
an item.

The Equipped Item database
number is loaded in *Variable
129:Weapon Equipped* to
*Variable 133:Accessory
Equipped.*

Flag 121:Action Status is on if
the member is under an
abnormal action status.

IF NOT IN A BATTLE: *Flag
180–189 Normal Flag,
Variable 180–189 Normal
Variable,* and *Input
018:Normal Input Variable* are
affected.

IF IN A BATTLE: *Flag 190–199
Battle Flag, Variable 190–199
Battle Variable,* and *Input
019:Battle Input Variable* are
affected.

SUBSTITUTE VARIABLE FOR ATTRIBUTE

This command allows you
to substitute variables for
the applicable target's
attributes. Using the target's
information and the status
of *Flag 081:Stat Check Type,* the
following data is outputted:

Variable 099:Strength

Variable 100:Defend

Variable 101:Intelligence

Variable 102:Agility

Variable 103:Luck

Variable 104:Attack

Variable 105:Armor

Variable 106:Max Hit Points

*Variable 107:Max Magic
Points*

The above figures are
corrected if *Flag 081:Stat Check
Type* is on. If the flag is off,
the figures are not corrected
(except Attack and Armor).
The status of *Flag 081:Stat
Check Type* does not affect:

Variable 097:Hit Points

Variable 098:Magic Points

IF NOT IN A BATTLE: *Flag
180–189 Normal Flag,
Variable 180–189 Normal
Variable,* and *Input 018:
Normal Input Variable* are
affected.

IF IN A BATTLE: *Flag 190–199
Battle Flag, Variable 190–199
Battle Variable,* and *Input 019:
Battle Input Variable* are
affected.

ITEM ACTION

This command allows you
to buy, sell, or use an item.
Selecting "Buy" adds the
item to the party's possessions and decreases the
party's money. The Items
database number is loaded
in *Variable 134:Item Number.*
The quantity of items
purchased is entered in
Variable 006:Item Quantity. The
item's price is entered in
Variable 007:Item Price.

If the item is placed in the
bag, *Flag: 003:Bag Shop Select*
turns on. If the item goes to
a member, the flag turns off.
The Member database
number of whoever receives
the item is entered in
Variable 086:Member Number.

Selecting "Sell" takes the
item from the party's
possession and increases
the party's money. You can
only sell one item at a time.
The Item's database number
is entered in *Variable 134:Item
Number.* The selling price is
loaded in *Variable 007:Item
Price.* Selling an item from

the bag switches *Flag 003:Bag Shop Select* on, while selling it from a member turns it off. The Member database number of the seller is entered in *Variable 086:Member Number.*

Selecting "Use" decreases the item from the party's possession. The item's database number is entered in *Variable 134:Item Number.* Using an item from the bag switches *Flag 003:Bag Shop Select* on; if a member uses an item, the flag turns off. The Member database number of the user is entered in *Variable 086:Member Number.*

GET MEMBER NAME

This allows you to get a member's name. The name of the member whose database number is entered in *Variable 086:Member Number* will be entered in *Input 001:Common Name.*

GET ENEMY NAME

This allows you to get an enemy's name. The name of the enemy whose database number is entered in *Variable 055:Enemy Battle Order* will be entered in *Input 001:Common Name.*

GET CLASS NAME

This allows you to get a class name. The name of the class the database number of which is entered in *Variable 088:Class Number* will be entered in *Input 001:Common Name.*

GET CLASS TITLE NAME

This allows you to get a class title's name. The name of the class title the database number of which is entered in *Variable 088:Class Number* and the level of which is entered in *Variable 090:Class Rank* will be entered in *Input 001:Common Name.*

GET TRAIT NAME

This allows you to get a trait's name. The name of the trait the database number of which is entered in *Variable 058:Trait Number* will be entered in *Input 001:Common Name.*

GET ITEM NAME

This allows you to get an item's name. The name of the item the database number of which is entered in *Variable 134:Item Number* will be entered in *Input 001:Common Name.*

GET ABILITY NAME

This allows you to get an ability name. The name of the ability the database number of which is entered in *Variable 155:Ability Number* will be entered in *Input 001: Common Name.* However, if the Ability database number is entered in *Variable 161:Random Ability Number*, that number has priority and that ability is used.

CONFIRM PARTY ITEM

Confirms the party's possession of the item designated by *Variable 134:Item Number.* If the party has the item, the quantity of the item in the bag is entered in *Variable 80:Total Items.*

CONFIRM MEMBER ITEM

Confirms that the party member in *Variable 086:Member Number* possesses the item designated by *Variable 134:Item Number.*

CONFIRM MEMBER ABILITY

Confirms that the member designated by *Variable 086:Member Number* has the ability designated by *Variable 155:Ability Number.* If so, *Flag 112:Has Magic* turns on.

DATABASE NUMBER FOR VARIABLE

This command allows you to insert a specified database number from a specified database into a designated variable. If database numbers later change, the numbers are automatically updated, provided you used this Script Command.

BATTLE ACTION

Allows you to set up an action in *Variable 060:Action: Action.*

SCRIPT BRANCH

These commands relate to the flow of the script.

CONDITION: If the designated condition is met, the Script Commands up to the Condition End will be executed. If the condition is not met, they will be passed by.

REPEAT: The Script Commands up to the Condition End will repeat while the designated conditions are met.

SORT: This command allows you to branch the script, allowing for multiple scenarios. Insert this command, then use the Apply If command for each case until you reach Script Branch End.

APPLY IF: Multiple scenarios are possible if the Apply If conditions are met as outlined in the Sort command.

NO APPLICATION: If the Apply If condition is not met, this command is used. In the in-game example, "What? That's not the password" is the "No Application."

TO END: This command takes you to the Script Branch End when the conditions within a Repeat or Sort script branch are fulfilled. In the in-game example, "To End" is entered after the correct password is given.

TO TOP: Takes you to the beginning of the script, just before Repeat or Sort is specified. Using the in-game example again, a wrong answer could have triggered a To Top command and the player would be asked for the password repeatedly until he entered it correctly.

Read the in-game Help text to see an example of script branching.

SCRIPT

These commands relate to the way scripts begin and end.

CALL SCRIPT: Allows you to call for a script and insert it within another script. If you make changes to the called script at a later time, all scripts that call for the changed script are automatically updated.

WAIT FOR SCRIPT END: Tells the system to wait for all called scripts to finish executing before the script continues. Use this command only if you used the Apply Together Script Command.

APPLY IN ORDER: Changes the Script execution method so that each Script Command is applied one after the other. This is the default method. There is no need to use this command unless you used the Apply Together command.

APPLY TOGETHER: Changes the Script execution method so that each Script Command after this command is executed at the same time, rather than one by one.

FORCE SCRIPT END: Forcibly cancels the script. Called scripts are not canceled, however.

NOTE

Script Commands within these menus are preceded by icons. A "globe" icon signifies that the command can only be used on the world map. A "sword" icon signifies that the command can only be used in battle. An icon of a sword and a globe signifies that the command can be used both on the world map and in battle. If the icon is highlighted (it will have a black background), the Script Command can be executed simultaneously with another script using the "Script/ Apply Together" command. If the icon has a white background the Script Command cannot be applied simultaneously. Finally, a command with no icon indicates that the command can be used in both the world and in battle, but it cannot be applied together with another command.

BATTLE

These scripts relate to battle flow.

ENEMY

These commands control enemy action during battle.

CALL SAME ENEMY: Calls the same enemy into battle. The called enemy acts as part of the enemy's group. For the call to succeed there must be fewer than 98 enemies and enough space for the display when the call succeeds. *Flag 113:Call Same Enemy* must be on.

CALL OTHER ENEMY: Allows the calling of a different, specified enemy. It acts as its own group in battle. There must be fewer than 98 enemies total, fewer than three groups, and room for the display when the call succeeds. *Flag 113:Call Same Enemy* must be on.

ENABLE CALL SAME ENEMY: Allows you to check whether the same enemy can be called to join the enemy party. When you can call, *Flag 113:Call Same Enemy* is on.

ENABLE CALL OTHER ENEMY: Allows you to check whether a different, specified enemy can be called to join the enemy party. When you can call, *Flag 113:Call Same Enemy* is on.

ENEMY ACTION: Allows you to apply a specified enemy action. If you set a marker in the Enemy Action Editor, the next Script Command will not begin until the action reaches that marker. However, if the Apply Together command is on, the next command will begin as soon as the action is generated, regardless of the marker.

DEFAULT ENEMY ACTION: Allows you to set up the action that you specified in "Enemies/Enemies/Adv/Status Set." The default action will be shown after the current action is finished.

ENEMY ACTION STILL: Allows you to stop and resume the current enemy action.

SYSTEM

This menu includes commands that control the battle system. A few definitions are prudent here. First, "Instigator" refers to the side that is taking action. The "Target" is the side receiving the "Action." For example, if you cast Heal on a party member, the party is both the instigator and the target. "Participant" can indicate either the instigator or the target. Finally, "Applicable"

indicates either the instigator or target that is the aim of the command.

NOTE

These are advanced battle settings and do not need to be used under normal circumstances. Attempt to use these only if you want to tweak the battle system.

CHECK WHO GOES FIRST: This command specifies the first instigator.

CHECK WHO GOES NEXT: Allows you to specify the next instigator.

CHANGE BACK ACTIVE CHARACTER: Allows you to switch back to the participant set up before the Direct Effect started.

SUBSTITUTE TARGET ATTRIBUTE FOR VARIABLE: Please refer to "Data/System/Substitute Attribute for Variable" above for detailed information.

SUBSTITUTE VARIABLE FOR TARGET ATTRIBUTE: Please see "Data/System/Substitute Variable for Target Attribute" above for detailed information.

MAKE ACTIVE CHARACTER: This command allows you to switch the instigator and the target.

GIVE EXP: Allows the party to receive the experience gained through battle. Input the targeted member's database number in *Variable 086:Member Number*. *Variable 020:Experience Received* is automatically entered when the battle ends. After the addition, the experience is entered in *Variable 095:Experience*.

GIVE MONEY: Allows the party to acquire money dropped by the enemy. The amount the enemy drops is automatically entered in *Variable 021:Money Received*, then added to *Variable 077:Total Party Money*.

GIVE ITEM: Allows you to acquire an item that the enemy drops. The dropped item's database number is entered in *Variable 134:Item Number*. If the enemy drops an item, *Flag 119:Receive Item* is turned on. If the flag is not turned on, nothing happens and both the variable and the flag are reset after the battle.

CHECK LEVEL UP: Increases by one a character's level after a battle. The targeted member's database number is entered in *Variable 086:Member Number*. If the character levels up, *Flag 115:Level Up* turns on. *Variable 091:Level* indicates the new level. The changed attributes are entered in *Variable 097:Strength* through *Variable 107:Max Magic Points*.

CHECK LEVEL UP AND ABILITY: Checks whether a member can gain a new ability with a level-up. The targeted member's database number is entered in *Variable 086:Member Number*. If the member learns a new ability, *Flag 116:Level Up & Ability* turns on. The database number of the ability is entered in *Variable 155:Ability Number*.

CHECK CLASS LEVEL UP: Checks whether a member can gain a new class level after the battle ends. The targeted member's database number is entered in *Variable 086:Member Number*. If the Class level goes up, *Flag 117:Class Level Up* turns on. The Class database number is entered in *Variable 088:Class Number*.

CHECK CLASS LEVEL UP AND ABILITY: Checks whether a member can gain a new ability after the class level goes up. The targeted member's database number is entered in *Variable 086:Member Number*. If a new ability is learned, *Flag 118:Class Level Up & Ability* turns on. The ability's database number is entered in *Variable 088:Class Number*.

OTHER

This is a miscellaneous menu that contains Script Commands not covered in the above menus.

EVENT BATTLE: This allows you to chose a specific place for a battle with a specified unit.

VEHICLE: Contains commands relating to vehicles.

SET AS VEHICLE: Allows you to register an event as a vehicle. You must set a number for each vehicle, because there is no database with which to manage them. The vehicle's location is automatically saved on the map.

RIDE VEHICLE: This command allows you to ride in this event and specify what type of vehicle it is.

DEPLOY VEHICLE: Allows you to choose the model for your vehicle.

CONTROL VEHICLE: Once you enter a vehicle, apply this command to control it.

EXIT VEHICLE: Allows you to exit a vehicle that you are controlling.

CALL VEHICLE: Allows you to specify the location of a designated vehicle.

CONTROLLER VIBRATION: This command makes the controller vibrate. You can also specify the strength and duration of the vibration here.

SHOW SAVE WINDOW: Displays a window that allows the player to save the game.

START NEW GAME FILE: Allows you to call for a different game data file from the same Memory Card.

WAIT: Allows you to wait a specified number of frames before the next command executes.

NONE: This command does nothing. Use it as a spacer to break up long scripts.

FINISH GAME: Ends the game.

NOTE: This command does nothing, but it does allow you to add notes to your script. For example, I might write: "Congratulations, you made it through this chapter!"

EVENTS

If you are confused by the number of Script Commands and their activities, relax. You'll have a better grasp on their usage after you familiarize yourself with events. Just remember that scripts make up events.

Understanding how events are created gives will lead you to a better understanding of scripts.

Enter the Event database by selecting "Scripts," then "Events" from the main menu. What you see are more than 360 pre-existing events for your use. Every event you need to create a unique game is here; it's up to you to decide how best to use them.

EVENT EDITOR

Select "Create New Data" to enter the Event Editor. If you followed the Sample Game Design, this screen is familiar to you, and you already know how to create a few events.

NAME: Enter a name for your event in this field.

NOTE: Enter a note in the Event Database.

TYPE: Select "Normal" for most events. You would select "System" if you were creating an event that dealt with the processing of system functions. For example, casting a fireball is a "Normal" event, but deciding how the damage is dealt is a "System" event. Only advanced users should attempt "System" events.

PAGE: Pages contain instructions on how an event is executed. For example, "Page 0" might occur if you speak to a villager. "Page 1" might occur the second time you speak to the villager, or if you are carrying a certain item. Pages are executed in order, from highest to lowest. Select "New" to create a new page to edit. "Copy," "Paste," and "Delete" refer to individual pages.

CONDITION TYPE: Selecting "Condition" allows you to set page conditions by selecting any of the 10 fields labeled "0" thru "9." Selecting "Script" allows for more detailed page conditions, but you must create a script first. Stick to "Condition" until you are familiar with creating detailed scripts.

0–9: Selecting any of these fields allows you to choose conditions for the execution of an event. For example, if a certain member is in the party, a villager may react with hostility.

DISPLAY TYPE: You select from "Character," "Object," or "Building." This determines what models are available in the "Model" field.

DIRECTION: Determine the direction the model is facing here. For example, you might want a treasure chest to open from the west, or an NPC to face east.

MODEL: Here you choose the model for your event. If you chose "Character" for the display type, the Character Model database is available.

MOTION: Call for an "Action" script type in this field. "Action" events run in the background automatically, without affecting player movement. For example, the flickering flames of a candle run continuously, but don't affect player movement. Apply the script for the flames in the "Motion" field.

START: This field allows you to specify how an event will start.

TOUCH: Select "Touch" if you want the event to start when the character comes in contact with it. If you have a villager run up to the leader, the event begins when they come in contact.

EQUAL: Select "Equal" when no model is used. Remember we set a warp event with Equal. The event starts when the character's location equals the event location.

TALK: Select "Talk" if you want the event to begin when you talk to a specified model.

EXAMINE: Select "Examine" if you want the event to begin when you examine the model. This could be as simple as a message that reads "Nothing was found" after an empty box is examined.

AUTO: Select "Auto" if the event begins automatically when the page conditions are met.

APPLY: Call up a script of the "Content" type within this field. The majority of your events will include scripts called out within this field.

NOTE

The second "Start" field is used to call up Script Commands that designate when the event starts. Script Commands can be far more detailed than the five options listed.

TIP

Within the Event database, select an event by highlighting it and pressing ✕. Select "Edit" to study how that event is laid out. Now move down to either the "Motion" or "Apply" field, whichever has a script called out, and tap ✕. The script is highlighted on a popup list. Tap ▲ and you're taken to the Script database. Tap ✕ and select "Edit" to read the contents of the script. When you are through, exit back to the Event database. This is an easy way to familiarize yourself with events and the scripts that make them up.

EVENT PLACEMENT

Once you create an event, it is saved to the Event database, ready for placement.

The Event Placement database contains Event Sets that will be registered within "Graphics/World Organization" to a certain map. For example, an event set for "My Dungeon" would be registered in World Organization to the map "My Dungeon." Only then would the events appear and work on the map.

Select "Create New Data" to enter the Event Placement Editor. Here is where you call up a specific map, and place all the events that you want on that map.

NAME: Enter a name for your Event Set. Remember, you are not naming an individual event, but a set that includes all the events that are to be placed on the map.

NOTE: Enter a note here. The note is seen only in the Event Placement database.

B DATA: Allows you to call up B Data for editing purposes. B Data is not saved, but it is useful if you want to call up an Event Set, copy portions of it, and use it for your new Set.

DATA: Choose either "Map Database" or "Dungeon Database," then call up a specific map. The map specified here is the map upon which you will place your events.

OBJECTS SET: If you created an Object Set for the map you specified in the "Data" box, select it here. This populates your map with whatever objects you placed within "Graphics/Object Placement."

EVENTS/MEMORY LEFT: This tells you how many events you can place and how much memory you have left to use.

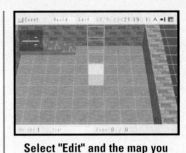

Select "Edit" and the map you specified loads. Move the cursor to the desired location and tap X to begin the placement process. Cycle through the events until you find the one you need and tap X again. Your event is placed. When you're finished, exit the Placement Editor and update your data. Your Event Placement Set is now registered in the Event Placement database. Remember, you need to register it in World Organization before the events are active in your game.

CHARACTER AND PARTY CREATION

CHARACTER MODEL MODIFICATION

The Character Models Editor allows you to customize the appearance of 115 pre-existing models. You can customize the appearance of a model—from animals to humans—for placement as either a party member or an NPC.

Enter the Character Model database by selecting "Graphics," then "Character Models" from the main menu. The database contains 115 models to choose from. Instead of altering the pre-existing models, let's create one of our own. Select the "Create New Data" button to enter the editor.

NAME: Select Name to enter a name for your character model.

NOTE: Any text entered here appears next to the model's name in the Character Model database. It does not appear in-game.

MODEL: Select "Model" field to choose your character's model. Scroll through the Character Model database and select a model that fits the role you have chosen for your new character.

COLOR: The Color field allows you to change the color of up to 16 areas of your model's appearance. Select one of the 16 small boxes and part of the model begins to blink, representing the area that is altered by changing the color.

TRANS: Increasing the value in the Trans box makes your model more transparent. At 100%, the character is invisible.

SIZE: Increase the percentage in "Size" to increase your character's size.

FACE: Select Face to choose one of 14 faces for your model.

PREVIEW: Highlight "Turn," then press and hold **✕** + the directional pad up/down/left/right to turn the model. Highlight the "Zoom" and "Move" buttons and manipulate your character in the same manner.

ACTION: Look at the Action field to see what actions your model can employ. These are for viewing only, and are not executed unless you set up a specific event that calls for the action.

LOOK: A model's Look is treated the same as its Action. An event must be created to use them.

NOTE

See the "Script and Event Creation" section for information on how to execute a Character Action. A character may have a "Special" action unique to that model. Make use of these actions to add flair to your adventure.

EDITING YOUR PARTY MEMBER

Creating a character model for use as an NPC was as easy as entering the Character Models Editor and tweaking a few superficial values. Creating a party member takes a little more work. Use the custom model you created earlier, and we'll start defining that character's role in your adventure.

To enter the Party Member database, select "Game," then "Party Members" from the main menu. Twenty party members in the database are ready to use. If you want to create a party member from scratch, select "Create New Data."

THE BASIC PAGE

Select "Basic" to name your party member and to choose a model for your character. You can use the model you created earlier, or any of the pre-existing models that suit your needs.

NOTE

Notice that your character's starting attribute values are listed, but they cannot be altered on this page.

THE CUSTOM PAGE

Select "Custom" to manipulate the member's stats, abilities, items, property, experience curve, titles, and info.

DETAILS

The Details page allows you to set your party member's sex, class, origin, bio, and unarmed attack.

SEX: Select "Sex2" through "Sex9" to denote a sex other than male or female. The generic names can be edited under "Game Settings/ Custom/Sex."

CLASS: Select a pre-existing class or keep it set to "-None-." You can create a unique class by selecting "Game," then "Classes" from the main menu. Once you do that, return to this page and pull up your unique class.

ORIGIN AND BIO: Write a unique origin or biography for your character.

NOTE

Make sure to input your "Bio" text so it appears as a one-line sentence in-game. Meaning, even though the input box is broken into two lines, just keep typing like it is all on one line.

PROPERTY: If the character is unarmed, this is its attack property. This has nothing to do with the actual Direct Effect associated with the attack, just the type of attack it is.

STATS

The Stats page lets you set the starting attribute values for your member, and the amount of increase per level gained.

TYPES: Select pre-existing templates here.

LEVEL 1: Select the starting values for the seven attributes of your member in the "Lvl 1" column.

LEVEL UP: In the "Lvl UP" column, set the amount each value increases with each level the member gains.

START LEVEL

"Start Lvl" allows you to choose the starting level for your character. The attributes increase by the values you set in the "Lvl UP" column in the Stats page.

EXPERIENCE CURVE

"Exp Curve" allows you to tweak how much experience is required for your character to level up. The maximum level a character can reach is 99.

NOTE

Use the blue and red buttons to clean up the experience between specified levels. For example, if you want it to take 10 experience points to gain Level 2 and 1,000 experience points to gain Level 99, you can set those values in the "Experience Required" column next to the appropriate level. The computer will fill in the intermediate level requirements automatically. First, highlight the "Lvl 2" row and select the blue button. Then, select the "Lvl 99" row and select the red button. It's as easy as that.

ABILITY

"Ability" allows you to set when and if the character gains abilities. If the "Lvl

Required" field contains a zero, the character never gains that ability.

NOTE

We create abilities later using the Abilities Editor. Once created, the abilities are automatically listed here.

ITEMS

The Items page allows you to specify what items a character starts the game with. Select up to 12, but note that if you want the character to begin the game with a weapon equipped, you have to equip it on the next page.

EQUIP

Specify here which items a character has equipped at the start of the game.

TITLE

This page lets you specify what class levels the character has attained at the start of the game. Selecting "-None-" denotes that the character has not gained any levels in the specified class. For more information on titles, see the Class Editor.

RESIST WEAPONS

"Resist W" lets you set your character's individual weapon resistances and vulnerabilities. For example, entering "50" in the Slash field cuts in half the damage taken by your member from a slashing weapon. On the other hand, entering "-50" would create a vulnerability to slashing weapons and increase damage by 50 percent.

RESIST MAGIC

"Resist M" allows you set up your character's individual magic resistances and vulnerabilities.

THE ADVANCED PAGE

The Advanced page allows a seasoned user to alter the way members act in combat, and even determine the flow of combat itself. The default settings should be adequate for the majority of users, so use caution when changing them.

TRAITS

The Traits page allows you to select the abnormal statuses and behavior of your character.

ACTION STATUS: Select a status here if you want your character to start the game with a certain condition. For example, if you select "Sleep," your character will start out with the Sleep Condition.

CUSTOM STATUS: Select a status here if you want the character to have a special attribute, such as the ability to regenerate health points or magic points.

TRAIT: Selecting a trait specifies how the member acts in combat. For example, select "Heal" to have the character heal every turn. If you set a trait here, you cannot control the character's actions in combat.

COMBAT

"Combat" allows you to set attack and defense effects for the member.

ATTACK (NO WEAPON)

NAME: The name you set here appears on the combat menu as the attack selection.

DIRECT EFFECT: Select a direct effect to occur when the character scores a hit without a weapon. For example, selecting "000:Fire" inflicts 15 base damage on a single target. It is also a magic attack.

INDIRECT EFFECT: After selecting a direct effect, you can select an indirect effect to apply after a successful hit.

DEFEND

NAME: The name you set here appears on the combat menu as the defend selection.

DIRECT EFFECT: A selection here determines what happens when this character defends. For example, you could have it cut damage in half.

INDIRECT EFFECT: Choose an indirect effect that occurs after the character has defended. For example, choose "0021: Attack +50" if your character is a Berserker type that gets upset if attacked.

DIRECTING

The "Directing" page calls for scripts that determine the flow of encounters.

ENCOUNTER FLOW

BATTLE START: During the start of battle, the system calls to each member individually and will execute whenever script is set here. For example, you could add opening battle dialogue here for each character.

BATTLE END: A script selected here executes at battle's end. You may wish your character to automatically recover health points or be cured of poison.

BATTLE FLOW

NORMAL/CRITICAL/DEFENSE/ OTHER/DODGE: This is where you set what happens when the character is in battle and one of these five situations occur. Typically, you would set sound and/or visual effects here.

NOTE

These events are also set within the Direct Effects Editor.

THE CONDITION PAGE

On this page, select a condition status type that you want your character to have at the start of the game. For example, you might create a minigame that begins with a party member being poisoned. The group must quickly find a cure before he expires.

MODEL SET

Here, you change a character's model to reflect any indirect effects they are suffering from. For example, you can create a model of your character with a green face to signify that he is poisoned.

FLAG

The "World" and "Battle" tabs allow you to switch on flags that can be used in the world or in battle. To use any of these flags, you must create a script command within an event. To do so, enter the Scripts Editor by selecting "Scripts/Scripts/Create New Data" from the main menu. Select the script box and "Data," then "Flags" from the dropdown menu.

VARIABLES

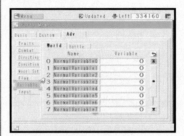

The "World" and "Battle" tabs also allow you to set variables that can be called up for use within the world or in battle. To call up any of these variables, create a Script Command within an event. To do so, enter the Scripts Editor by selecting "Scripts/Scripts/Create New Data" from the main menu. Select the script box and "Data," then "Variable" from the dropdown menu.

INPUT

Enter in the "Text Variable" column any text that you want to pull up using a script command. To call up these inputs, enter the Scripts Editor by selecting "Scripts/Scripts/Create New Data" from the main menu. Select the script box and "Data," then "Input" from the dropdown menu.

NOTE

More information on scripts and events can be found in the "Script and Event Creation" section.

GENERAL SETTINGS

The next step is to register your party, and select their starting point. The General Settings menu also allows you to customize several settings for your adventure.

Enter General Settings by selecting "Game," then "General Settings" from the main menu.

THE BASIC PAGE

On this page, choose your starting party members, their collective money, and their starting location.

PARTY

You can choose from one to four party members by selecting the appropriate field, then selecting a character from the Party Member database. Any character that you created in "Game"/"Party Members" is available for selection. Select "-None-" if you want to create a party smaller than four. Use the arrow buttons to change the order of your party.

MONEY

Highlight this field to change the amount of gold with which your party begins.

LOCATION

Select the "Location" field to choose your party's starting map. All maps registered in "Graphics"/"World Organization," are available to choose.

To specify an exact location, select the placement button and the map you just selected loads. Move the cursor to the place you would like your party to start, and press X. Press SELECT to exit the map.

THE CUSTOM PAGE

On this page, customize starting possessions and encounter settings.

BAG

Check the "Enable Item Bag" box if you want your party to start out with an item bag. Uncheck the box if you want your characters to start the game solely with their own inventories.

ITEMS

If you selected "Enable Item Bag" on the "Bag" page, you can select what items appear within the bag on this page.

BATTLE

SCREEN EFFECT: Change how the World Map transitions to the battle screen by selecting "Screen Effect."

BGM: The BGM field allows you to change the background music that plays during battles.

WORLD SOUNDS: Selecting "World Sounds" allows you to change the environmental sounds that play during battle.

ENCOUNTER: Alter the party's chances of encountering a battle per step. The default value is a 10 percent chance.

THE ADVANCED PAGE

Set font attributes, detailed encounter ratios, and flags, variables, and inputs on this page.

FONT

Set the general type, size, and color of the in-game text here. Employ scripts to alter these settings throughout your game. Note that changing the font size might adversely affect how some of the preset scripts display text.

Most of the preset scripts were designed to allow font size increases, but some were not. Also, you should determine the desired font size prior to creating your game to ensure that inputted text displays correctly.

ENCOUNTER

You may have set the overall encounter ratio in "Custom/Battle," but this page allows you to tweak the percent chance of the party entering a battle per a set number of steps. For example, set "Steps 1–5" to zero% if you don't want your party to enter any battles for at least five steps.

Flag

This page allows you to set flag positions at the start of the game. You can then use Script Commands to make the system take certain actions depending on the position of certain flags. For example, picking up a quest item might turn a switch "On". Then, when the party speaks to a certain villager, the villager might divulge more information only if that flag is "On" (meaning they completed the quest). See the Script and Event Creation chapter for more information.

Variable

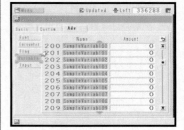

Variables are number "containers" that store anything from member attributes to bank account balances. You can add a number to a variable here and then call it up using Script Commands. You can then use that number in any way you choose.

Input

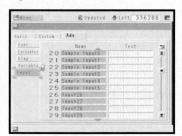

Inputs are just like variables except they deal with text rather than numbers. You can add text to an unused Input here, then call it up whenever necessary with the appropriate Script Command.

USING THE CLASS EDITOR

The "Classes" menu lets you create a new class from scratch or alter a pre-existing class to fit your needs.

Enter the Class database by selecting "Game," then "Classes" from the main menu. You have 11 pre-existing classes to work with. If you want to start from scratch, select "Create New Data." If you want to alter an existing class, select it from the database, then select "Copy" and "Paste Copied Data."

THE BASIC PAGE

Name your class by entering text within the "Name" field. The "Note" field allows you to create a note that is listed next to the class name in the Class database.

THE CUSTOM PAGE

This page lets you customize the details, stats, abilities, and overall progression of the class.

DETAIL

In "Description," enter a description for your class. Check the "Conceal Description" box to hide the description in-game. This information shows up when you use the "Display Class Info" Script Command.

PROMOTE

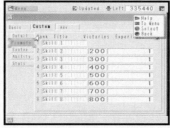

This page allows you to set ranks for your class. You can also set the prerequisites for gaining each new rank/title in terms of victories and/or experience.

EVOLVE

You can set up the class so that you must achieve certain ranks in other classes before you can become this class.

ABILITY

This page allows you to set the abilities that a character can acquire as he rises through the ranks of his class.

STATS

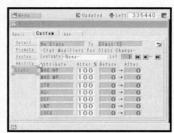

This page allows you to set how a character's attributes are altered when they join a certain class. For instance, a character who becomes a fighter may gain a significant number of "Max HP" and "STR." Select a character to "Evaluate" and you can see how their stats change as they gain levels.

THE ADVANCED PAGE

Advanced options deal with special class abilities that you can set.

CLASS INDIRECT EFFECT: Set an indirect effect for your class. For example, a member of a Druidic class may draw magic points from their surroundings at every step.

CLASS START: Set an event that occurs when the character takes the class.

CLASS END: Set an event that occurs when a character drops the class.

BATTLE VICTORY: Set an event that occurs when the character achieves a victory in battle.

ENEMY CREATION

OVERVIEW OF ENEMY CREATION

Creating your enemy takes several steps. The first step involves editing the enemy model to your taste. Within the Enemy Model Editor, you can create and name a new enemy model, as well as alter an enemy's outward appearance.

Next, we visit the Enemy Actions Editor and create the animations the enemy can perform.

In the Enemy Editor, you name the enemy, tweak its stats, and set its resistances, vulnerabilities, and drops.

The Unit Editor allows you to specify whether or not the enemy appears as part of a larger unit. It also allows you to test the enemy in a mock battle against your party.

Finally, the Unit Placement page lets you designate where your enemies and units appear, and how often they are encountered.

EDITING AN ENEMY MODEL

The Enemy Models Editor lets you customize the appearance of 103 pre-existing models, from Arch Demons to Zombies.

Enter the Enemy Model database by selecting "Graphics," then "Enemy Models" from the main menu. The database contains 103 models. Create a new model from scratch by selecting "Create New Data" or alter a pre-existing model by selecting it, selecting "Copy," then selecting "Paste Copied Data."

ENEMY MODEL EDITOR

This page is almost identical to the Character Model Editor, so those of you familiar with creating characters should find no surprises here.

NAME: Select the "Name" field to enter a name for your enemy model.

NOTE: Any text entered here appears next to the model's name in the Enemy Model database. It does not appear in-game.

MODEL: Select "Model" to choose your enemy's model. Scroll through the Enemy Model list and select a model that fits your needs.

COLOR: The Color field allows you to change the color of up to 16 areas of your model's appearance. Select one of the 16 small boxes and part of the model begins to blink. The blinking part represents the area to be altered by the color change.

TRANS: Increasing the value in the "Trans" box makes your model more transparent. At 100%, the model becomes invisible.

SIZE: Increase the percentage in the "Size" field to increase your enemy's size.

PREVIEW: Highlight the "Turn" button, then press and hold ✗ + directional pad up/down/left/right to turn the model. Highlight the "Zoom" and "Move" buttons and manipulate your character in the same manner.

ACTION: Within the "Action" field, see what actions and attacks your model can employ. These are for viewing only, and are not executed unless you set up actions in the Enemy Action Editor (See "Enemy Actions" below).

ENEMY ACTIONS

Now that you have your model, select the actions that it will employ. You can choose to use preset actions, or create new and unique actions from scratch using the Enemy Action Editor.

Select "Enemies," then "Enemy Actions" from the main menu to bring up the Enemy Action database. If you created an enemy model earlier, it will not show up within this database just yet.

You can allow your custom model to emulate any of the other 103 enemy attacks. For example, if you altered the Slime model, but you don't like the Slime's attacks, you can choose for the Slime to emulate the Ogre attacks. Select a creature from the database and select "Copy." Then select "Paste Copied Data" to enter the Enemy Action Editor.

THE BASIC PAGE

Select a name for your enemy actions and compose a note to be placed in the database. Select either a pre-existing model or your custom model within the "Model" field. Remember, you don't have to select the model type that is identical to the enemy action you selected in the Enemy Action database.

NOTE

By copying and pasting an enemy action from the Enemy Action database, you have already set the actions for your custom enemy. Exit the editor after you name your enemy and call up the desired model. The "Edit" tab is optional, and only used to create a custom action.

THE EDIT PAGE

This page allows you to view your model's attacks and compose new attacks from pre-existing data.

TYPE: Select the type of action you would like to view or edit here.

COPY: Select the "Copy" button to copy the action displayed in the "Type" field.

PASTE: After you have copied an action, select a generic action from the "Type" field and press "Paste." The generic action will become the pasted action. The paste feature not only allows you to copy and paste actions within the current enemy action, but also allows you to paste them into other enemy's actions. This allows you to compile new enemy actions from multiple enemy actions.

PLAY AND STOP ICONS: Select the green play button to see your enemy perform the action in the preview window.

VIEW: Select this button to view the action up close and personal.

NOTE

If you selected "Create New Data" at the Enemy Action database, nothing happens when you select an action to view. You have to create a new motion before your enemy attacks.

CREATE A CUSTOM ACTION

We'll take you through the process of editing a couple of pre-existing attacks into one custom attack using the Motion Editor.

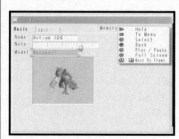

From the Enemy Action database, select "Create New Data." On the Basic page, select the Werewolf within the Model field.

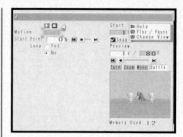

Select the "Edit" tab and change the "Type" to "Attack A."

NOTE

Because we selected "Create New Data," "Attack A" is an empty action that is ready for creation. Had we copied an action and selected "Paste Copied Data," "Attack A" would already have an action set to it. In this case, you should select a generic "Type" to edit ("Enemy Action05" for instance).

TIP

Change any of the Action names in "Game/Game Settings/Adv/Action."

Move your cursor down to "Motion" and tap **X**. Select "New" from the pulldown menu to open the Motion Editor. Select "Attack B" as the motion (this is one of the actual movements that are preset to the Werewolf model). Check out this motion by pressing the play button. You should see the Werewolf howl followed by another short animation. Update and exit the Motion Editor.

Now add another motion at frame 38 of "Attack B." Press the R1 button or move the cursor over to the slider bar (over "Marker") and change the current frame to 38.

NOTE

Changing the frame value to 38 creates a work frame at frame 38. If you want to create another work frame in the future, when using the other editors, use the same process to change the frame.

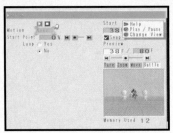

Select "Motion" once again and select "New." You notice the Werewolf is still frozen at frame 38. Select "Attack A" as the motion this time to insert the "Attack A" animation at frame 38 of the "Attack B" animation. Update your data and exit the Motion Editor.

To finish, increase the overall length of the action by moving over to the white box with the "80" in it. Change "80" to "121."

View your creation by pressing the play button or pressing the "View" button (full screen). To stop the animation, select the stop button or press ▲.

NOTE

Once you understand the Motion Editor, the other 13 editors will be straightforward. If you need help, press START> wherever you get stuck.

CUSTOMIZING YOUR ENEMY

Finally you get to put the pieces together. First you chose your enemy's model or customized one to suit your style. Then you selected your enemy's actions. Now all you need to do is name your enemy and the creation process is complete. Of course, as in all the other editors in *RPG Maker 2*, you can choose to do much more in the Enemy Editor than just name your creature.

To access the Enemy database, select "Enemies," then "Enemies" from the main menu. Select "Create New Data" and the Enemy Editor screen pops up.

THE BASIC PAGE

This page allows you to name your enemy, scribe a note that appears in the Enemy database, and call up the enemy action you created earlier. Once you've named your enemy and called up an action, the enemy appears in the Enemy database, ready for placement.

THE CUSTOM PAGE

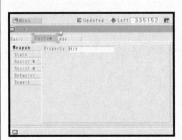

This page allows you to set the attack, statistics, resistances, behavior, and reward for the enemy.

WEAPON

Selecting "Property" dictates the type of damage the enemy inflicts on a successful hit.

STATS

Set the enemy's attributes on this page. Should you want to compare the enemy's stats with a party member's stats, select the party member in the "Compare" field.

RESIST WEAPON

Here you set the enemy's resistance or vulnerabilities to weapon attack types.

RESIST MAGIC

Here you set the enemy's resistance or vulnerabilities to magic attack types.

BEHAVIOR

Here you customize how the enemy behaves in combat. For example, you can make the enemy attack 100 percent of the time, or attack 50 percent, heal 25 percent, and defend 25 percent.

REWARD

This page lets you determine what rewards are given for defeating the enemy. You can set the amount of experience and money that the party acquires as well as any items that the creature may drop. The "Chest Ratio" indicates the percent chance that the party acquires a certain item. "Rare Chest Ratio" is the percent chance that the party receives a rare item. For example, if you set the Chest Ratio to 75 percent, and the Rare Chest Ratio to 25 percent, the party has about a 19 percent overall chance to acquire the rare item.

THE ADVANCED PAGE

This page is similar to the Advanced page in the Party Member Editor.

TRAITS

Select an Action Status or a Custom Status that the creature begins the game with. Select a trait to specify how the creature acts in battle. Be aware that selecting a trait here overrides the behavior you set on the Custom page.

COMBAT

Here you set the direct and indirect effects that occur when the creature attacks and defends.

DIRECTING

You can decide how the enemy reacts during combat on this page. A "Battle Start" Script is used when you want something to occur before the battle starts. Pull up a Script within the "Battle End" field to direct an enemy's action after it dies. Entering Scripts within the field under "Battle Flow" direct the enemy in combat.

CONDITION

You can select up to nine indirect effects for your enemy on this page. Conditions are any effects that raise or lower attributes. For example, you can set an "Increase Armor" effect or "Decrease Attack" effect.

STATUS SET

This page allows you to set the action displayed for different Action Statuses, such as dead or paralyzed. You set the priority values in the "Priority" field.

All indirect effects have priority numbers already attached to them. View these by entering the Indirect Effects database ("Game/Indirect Effects"). If you want your creature to display a certain action when he is affected by "Numb," which has a priority of 500, set one of the status fields (there are 10) to 500 and pull up the action you want displayed.

> **NOTE**
>
> You can create unique actions to fit your statuses within the Enemy Action Editor.

> **NOTE**
>
> See the help screens in "Game/Indirect Effects/Custom/Settings/Priority" and "Game/Party Members/Adv/Model Set" for more information.

FLAG

On this page, switch on flags that can be used in battle. To use any of these flags, you must create a script command within an event. To do so, enter the Scripts Editor by selecting "Scripts/Scripts/Create New Data" from the main menu. Then, select the script box and select "Data," then "Flags" from the dropdown menu.

VARIABLE

This page allows you to set variables that can be called up for use in battle. To call up any of these variables, you must create a script command within an event. To do so, enter the Scripts Editor by selecting "Scripts/Scripts/Create New Data" from the main menu. Select the script box and select "Data," then "Variable" from the dropdown menu.

INPUT

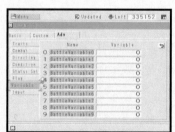

Enter text in the "Text Variable" column that you want to pull up using a Script Command. To call up these inputs, enter the Scripts Editor by selecting "Scripts/Scripts/Create New Data" from the main menu. Select the script box and select "Data," then "Input" from the dropdown menu.

NOTE

More information on scripts and events can be found in the "Script and Event Creation" section.

CREATING A UNIT SET

At this point you have probably created only a single enemy, but you still need to specify it as a unit so you can choose where it appears.

Select "Enemies," then "Units" from the main menu to enter the Units database. You can select to alter, copy, or create a new Unit Set from here. We selected "Create New Data" to build a Unit Set from scratch.

THE BASIC PAGE

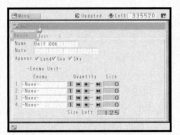

The Basic page is straight-forward. Fill out the "Name" field with an appropriate Unit Set name. Text entered

in the "Note" field appears next to the Unit Set name in the Units database. Check or uncheck the "Land," "Sea," and "Sky" boxes to specify whether you encounter your unit on land, in a boat, or in the air.

Use the four fields in the "Enemy" column to set your custom enemy, a pre-existing enemy, or a mix of both. You can also specify how many enemies of each type you want to appear by entering a value in the "Quantity" column. Your only limit is the size of each unit.

THE TEST PAGE

The Test page allows you to set up a mock battle between your party and your Unit Set. Select up to four members in the "Party" column, then choose the battlefield where you want to do battle.

Should you want to give your party members a leg up, select the "Member" pages and equip them for battle, or increase their level to raise their stats.

Once you have adequately balanced your enemy Unit Set, exit the editor and update your data. The Unit Set now appears in the Units database, ready for placement.

UNIT PLACEMENT

All that is left is to choose where and how often your enemy unit appears. Enter the Unit Placement database by selecting "Enemies," then "Unit Placement" from the main menu. Select "Create New Data" to place your unit on a custom map.

THE BASIC PAGE

This page allows you to register a Unit Set on a particular map.

DETAILS

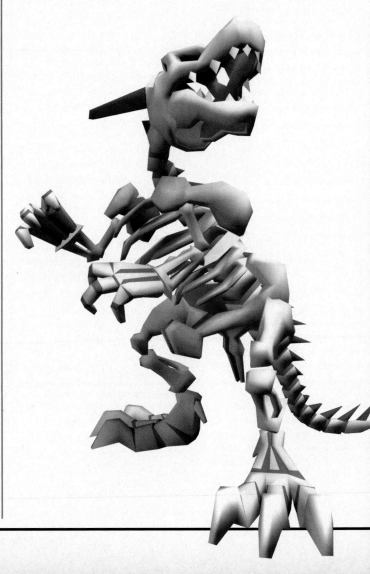

Click on the Details page to name the entire Unit Set that appears on a given map. If you create 20 individual units in the Units Editor, they can all be set to appear on one map within Unit Placement.

After you've named your Unit Set and added a note (optional), choose on which map you would like your Unit Set to appear. Note that you can only choose the appearance locations of individual units on world maps, within dungeons, they appear on the entire map.

UNITS

The Units page allows you to register up to 100 units to be placed on the map you specified on the "Details" page. You may augment your created units with pre-existing ones from the database if you like.

RATIO

You can now determine how often you would like each unit you selected on the Units page to appear. The higher the ratio entered, the more frequently a unit appears.

TIP

Use a low ratio for a unique enemy and make sure it carries a rare treasure. This makes anyone who plays your game want to undertake encounter after encounter until they find the creature and gain the prize.

EDIT

Select the "Edit" button to enter the Unit Placement Editor and place your units on the specified map.

NOTE

Remember, you cannot specify placement locations within dungeons; the Units you specify will appear throughout the entire dungeon. Use the "Other/Event Battle" Script Command if you want to create a battle at a specified location within a dungeon (or a map).

UNIT NAME: Check the box next to the Unit you wish to place on the map. Check as many Units as you want to appear in a single area.

APPEAR: Of the checked Units, this is how many appear on land, in the sea, or in the sky. You chose these location preferences in the "Unit Editor." If you choose a location on the map that includes land, sea, and sky, only units that can appear in each location will. For instance, a "land" creature will never appear in the sea, even if the sea is selected.

PLACE: Select the "Place" button to place the Units you checked in the "Unit Name" column. A green cursor will appear on the map. Move the cursor to the desired location and press ✗. Use the directional pad to increase the size of the box as desired. Press ✗ again to set the placement area. A colored box will remain, showing that units have been placed in that area.

DELETE: Select the "Delete" button to remove all or part of a placement area.

ALL UNITS APPEAR/ NOT ALL UNITS APPEAR: The semi-transparent box that appears on the map after you finalize a placement area will be one of two colors. The color will match either the "All Units Appear" color or the "Not All Units Appear" color. "All Units Appear" indicates that all of the checked Units appear within that placement area. "Not All Units Appear" indicates that none or more (but not all) of the Units appear in the placement area.

NOTE

After Placement is complete, visit the World Organization page to call up the Unit Set on your dungeon or World Map. They don't appear until you do so.

ITEMS DATABASE

EDITING ITEMS

Using the Item database, you can alter the names and effects of existing items or create new items from scratch. View and customize more than 100 items, weapons, and armor pieces here. To enter the database, select "Game," then "Items" from the main menu.

THE BASIC PAGE

The Basic page allows you to alter a pre-existing item name or enter a name for a created item. You can also alter or add a note for personal reference. The "Type" field can only be changed within "Custom/Type."

THE CUSTOM PAGE

On the Custom page, customize many aspects of the item you are creating. You can set the selling price, create effects that the item has on the user, specify who can use or equip the item, and more.

NOTE

Notice that only the sub-menus relevant to the item type are available.

DETAIL

The Detail page lets you add or alter the item's description and set options related to the item's value.

DESCRIPTION: The description you enter here appears when the item is examined in-game. Select "Conceal Description" to hide the in-game description. Note that item descriptions are displayed two ways in-game: one single line (in battle) and split between three lines (in world). When inputting text, make sure to type it so that it will display properly on three lines (the game system will add or remove spaces so that it will display properly when displayed on one line).

BUY: Set the price of the item here.

SELL: The sell price is determined automatically by the Sell Ratio.

SELL RATIO: Set this so the item will sell for a percentage of the buy price. If you enter 50%, for example, this item will be sold back for half of its buy price.

CAN NOT SELL: Check this box and the item cannot be sold.

CAN NOT DISCARD: Check this box and the item cannot be discarded. This is a fail-safe so you cannot get rid of items necessary to complete the game.

NOTE

If a member leaves the party holding an item that has been marked "Can Not Discard," the item is automatically placed in the party's bag. To make that item available, however, you must check "Enable Item Bag" in "Game/General Settings/ Custom/Bag." If you don't have "Enable Item Bag" checked, your party can still access the bag at any time if you use the Script Command "Script/ Party/Possessions/ Use Bag."

TYPE

The Type page allows you to select the type of item you are creating. Different options become available depending upon the type you choose.

USED

Here you can apply Direct and Indirect Effects that occur when the item is used.

EQUIPPED

This page allows you to set attribute bonuses and penalties when the item is equipped. The "Attack" value gives a bonus or penalty to your attack in battle. The "Armor" value applies a bonus or penalty to your

armor in battle. Use the "Indirect Effect" field to apply an Indirect Effect to the item when equipped.

MEMBERS

Determine here which members can equip the item. If "Remove" is not checked, members cannot remove the item once it's equipped.

CLASSES

Determine which classes can equip the item on this page. Make sure "Remove" is checked so the party member can remove the item once it has been equipped.

ATTACK

This page is only available if you chose "Weapon" on the "Type" page. Here, set the Direct Effect of the weapon, which is the damage it does right away. You also can set the Indirect Effect, which is any lingering effect that a weapon deals. And you can set the Property, which is the type of damage the weapon deals.

NOTE

When you create enemies, you set their resistances and vulner- abilities to certain types of damage in "Enemies/ Enemy Editor/Resist M or Resist W." If you want a weapon to be useful against a certain type of enemy (all undead enemies, for example), you would set the Property of the weapon to one that the enemy is particularly vulnerable to.

THE ADVANCED PAGE

The Advanced page allows you to set events that occur when the item is equipped, sold, or discarded. For example, equipping a certain item might cause an item to appear or even make the party warp elsewhere.

THE TRAITS DATABASE

The Traits database is a relatively small database that includes customizable traits that direct your party member's and/or enemy's behavior during combat.

NOTE

Refer to "Game/Party Members/Adv/Traits" to apply a trait to a party member.

THE BASIC PAGE

Select a trait to edit, or select "Create New Data" to make this screen appear. The Basic page allows you to name your trait, and post a note in the database.

THE CUSTOM PAGE

The Custom page allows you to write a description and attach a Script Command to the trait.

VISUAL EFFECTS

EDITING VISUAL EFFECTS

The Visual Effects database has more than 160 visual effects that you can alter to your liking. From candle flames to lightning to falling weights, enough data already exists to create just about any effect you desire. You can also start from scratch by selecting "Create New Data." To access the Visual Effects database, select "Graphics," then "Visual Effects" from the main menu.

Select "Create New Data" from the database to get this page. Let's create an effect together so you get the hang of it. First, change the generic effect name to "Boomerang."

Next, move the cursor to the "end frame" box and select "299." Change the "299" to "40."

NOTE

Thirty frames equal one second, so this effect lasts just over one second.

Now, select "New Element" at the bottom of the page. From the popup menu that appears, select "Object/Weapons/Boomerang." The Element Setup screen appears.

Our boomerang looks good, but it is static. We need to make some changes so the boomerang acts like a boomerang in flight. Tap X to begin editing the boomerang.

To alter the "Rotate" field, select it, then choose "Z-Axis" from the dropdown list. Next, change the "Speed" to "10." There, that looks more realistic. Exit and update your data.

Now we have to create a flight path for our boomerang. Select the long, white rectangle to the right of "1 Boomerang." Choose "Edit" from the popup menu. Move the cursor to any frame you desire, using the directional pad. Notice that as you move the cursor left and right, the "Current Frame" box changes to indicate which of the 40 available frames you have selected.

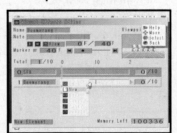

Select frame "0" and tap X. Select "New" from the menu to enter the Visual Effects Editor. At frame 0 (before any time has passed) we want our boomerang at its origin. We don't have to move the boomerang horizontally. We need to move it vertically, however, because the boomerang is now on the floor.

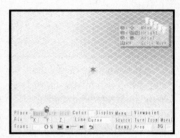

To bring the boomerang up to eye level, place the cursor over "Move" within the "Place" row. Hold down X and press L1 five or six times.

NOTE

To get a better perspective on the map, move the cursor over to the "Turn," "Zoom," and "Move" buttons at the right side of the screen. Hold X, select one of these buttons, and move the directional pad to change your viewpoint of the map. This makes it easier to judge how far you need to raise the boomerang.

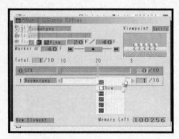

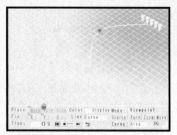

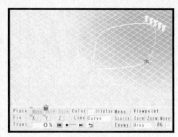

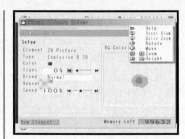

Once you have raised the boomerang to a more appropriate height, exit the editor and update your data. Notice that a blue box appears at frame 0, indicating that you edited that frame. Move the cursor to frame 20, halfway into our effect's duration. Tap ✕ and select "New" to re-enter the editor.

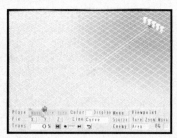

Halfway through our effect, we want the boomerang to contact the target. Move the boomerang straight across the grid to just in front of the group (they represent the target of the effect). You see a white line trailing the red cursor. This line represents the flight path of our boomerang. Exit the editor and update your data.

We all know that a boomerang does not travel in a straight line, so we need to create a curved trajectory. Move the cursor to frame 10 and tap ✕. Select "New" and you're back in the editor. Because we chose the tenth frame, halfway between the origin and the target, the red cursor appears in the middle of the white line. Move the boomerang left on the grid to create an arcing flight path.

NOTE

Look at the control panel within the editor and notice the "Line" field reads "Curve." If you changed it to "Straight," the boomerang's trajectory would not curve, but instead would look at this point like half of a 2-D diamond.

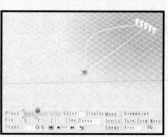

Exit the editor and select frame 40 to edit. Frame 40 represents the end of the effect, so place the boomerang back at its origin. The grid looks like this after you moved the red cursor back to the origin.

Finally, select frame 30 to edit. Complete the trajectory by moving the boomerang to the right of the grid. The white trajectory line should resemble a lemon when you are finished. If you want to create a more realistic path, edit frames 5, 15, 25, and 35. Moving those points out a bit creates a more rounded trajectory.

To see your boomerang in full-screen splendor, select "View." Tap ▲ to play and stop the animation. Highlight "Zoom," hold ✕, and press down on the directional pad to move the camera back past the boomerang's origin. You can now see its entire flight path.

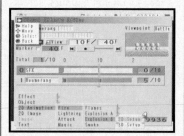

Now we should add a "hit" effect to signify that our boomerang struck its target. Select the "New Element" button, then select "2D Animation/Fire/Explosion B/2D Setup" from the dropdown menu.

We can now edit the "Explosion B" element. Select the "Color" field and choose a color for the explosion (we've chosen a deep red to simulate a wound, but feel free to choose any color). Now select "Normal" from the "Blend" field. The explosion takes on a deep crimson appearance. Finally, uncheck the "Repeat" box so our explosion only occurs once. Exit the Element Setup page and update your data.

Now to place the explosion: Highlight the frame field to the right of "Explosion B 2D" and tap ✕. Select "Edit" and place the green cursor at frame 20, exactly where the boomerang strikes the target. Tap ✕ and select "New" to enter the editor.

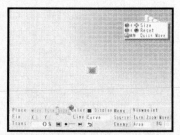

Wow, that's a big explosion! Tap the directional pad right twice to select "Size." Hold ✕ and press the directional pad left to decrease the size of the explosion. The white box that frames the red explosion should cover about four green boxes on the grid.

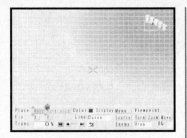

Once the explosion is a reasonable size, place it at the point of impact. Move the explosion to just in front of the target, using "Move" (the button next to "Place").

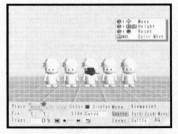

Now, highlight "Area" at the right of the tool bar. Tap ✗ and select "Battle." Move the explosion to the point of impact, directly in front of the target. Update your data and exit.

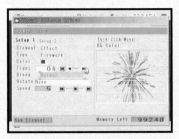

The effect looks pretty good, but let's add a little more character to it. Select "New Element," then "Effect/Firework." Within the "Setup1" page, change the color to the same red as the explosion. Now, select "Normal" within the "Blend" field.

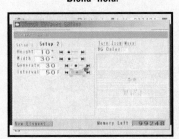

Select the "Setup2" page and change "Height" to 10 degrees, "Width" to 30 degrees, "Generate" to 30 and "Interval" to 50. Notice that the original effect looks a lot more like a wound now than it does fireworks. Update your data and exit.

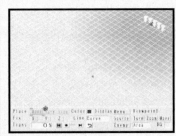

Now, place the "Firework" effect at the 20th frame and enter the editor to line it up. Once in the editor, move the effect from the origin to the target by switching "Battle" to "Area" and using the yellow "Move" button.

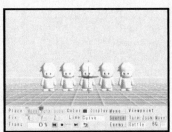

Once the red cursor is near the target, change "Area" back to "Battle." The effect is sitting on the floor. Hold ✗ with the yellow "Move" button selected, and press L1 until the wound lines up with the boomerang.

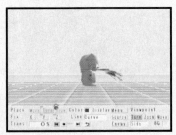

To verify that it is lined up, change "Battle" to "Side." Is the effect facing the wrong way? If so, highlight the yellow "Turn" button, hold ✗, and use the directional pad to make it "shoot" toward the point of origin. Update your data and exit.

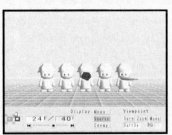

That's it! You've created your first visual effect. Play around with other effects, and you'll see that your designs are truly only limited by your imagination.

TIP

No visual effect is complete without sound effects. Edit the SFX field exactly as you did the Element fields. For the boomerang effect that we just created, add "084:Boomerang" to frame 0, "089:Crush" to frame 20, and "098:Splash 4" to frame 21.

IMPORTING AN IMAGE USING A DIGITAL CAMERA

Certain digital cameras allow you to download pictures directly into *RPG Maker II* for use as visual effects. To do so, connect a USB cable from your camera to the PS2 USB port. Select "Graphics/Image/ Create New Data." Now select "Get/Camera Image" and a thumbnail list of compatible pictures will load. Select the image you want, then save it as an image file. You can then use your image in countless ways. The picture can be used as a background in battle, or as wallpaper within an interior. You can use it as a logo or title screen, and even as a texture for a block. Furthermore, your camera should allow you to download images that are stored in your computer. These can be drawn pictures or manipulated photos. With creative uses of scripts, events, and visual effects, you can do just about anything with your digital images.

To access your saved image within the Visual Effects Editor, select "New Element/Image." You will be able to edit the image, and integrate it into a visual effect.

If you do not have a compatible camera, you can use the same process to alter a screenshot. Take a screenshot by pressing the right analog button R3 and the left analog button L3 simultaneously. Instead of selecting "Get /Camera Image" from "Graphics/ Image/Create New Data," select "Get/Screenshot," then save it as an image file. Note that only one screenshot is saved at a time.

THE ABILITIES DATABASE

The Abilities database contains more than 100 pre-existing abilities you may alter. Abilities consist of both magic and skills. All abilities call on Direct or Indirect Effects or both. Unless you are proficient with the use of scripts, it's best to customize pre-existing data rather than create new data. To enter the Abilities database, select "Game," then "Abilities" from the main menu.

THE BASIC PAGE

The Basic page allows you to change the name of the ability and make a note for reference. Change the "Type" and "Usable" fields on the Custom page.

THE CUSTOM PAGE

The Custom page allows you to change many aspects of the ability such as Type, Cost, and Effect. If you use pre-existing data, this page should remain unaltered.

TYPE: Select "Magic" or "Skill" here to place the ability in the respective in-game menu. This setting also determines the Status Type of the ability.

USABLE: This field determines where the ability can be used. A fireball, for example, can only be used in battle.

PROPERTY: The Property field allows you to set the property of the ability. A fireball's property is "Fire," and fire can affect enemies differently depending on the resistances you set up within "Enemies/Enemy Editor/Resist Magic."

COST: The value in the Cost field determines how many Magic Points the ability consumes. Check out "File 70:Consume MP1" to see how MP is consumed. You can change what is consumed by editing similar scripts.

DIRECT/INDIRECT EFFECT: Here you set the immediate effect (Direct Effect) and the lingering effect (Indirect Effect). You can call out custom Direct and Indirect Effects that you created in their respective editors.

DESCRIPTION: The in-game description of the ability. Check "Conceal" to hide the in-game description.

THE ADVANCED PAGE

The Advanced page lets you set your ability as a random ability, adding a percentage chance that a different ability will take effect instead of the ability used.

ENABLE AS RANDOM ABILITY: Check this to set the ability as a random ability. Using a random ability presents a chance that a different ability will be called up automatically. You set the percentage of that chance in the "Random Ratio" field.

ENABLE RANDOM EFFECT: This allows you to specify the percentage chance that the ability will be called by a random ability. Call out the ability in the "Random Ability" field that is able to call this ability randomly and a ratio in the "Random Ratio" field.

DISABLE ABILITY AS RANDOM: If this box is checked, using the ability does not trigger an additional ability.

DIRECT AND INDIRECT EFFECTS

DIRECT EFFECTS

The Direct Effect database contains 168 entries that can be viewed and altered to suit your needs. Direct Effects are effects that take place immediately after use, such as attacks and healing. To enter the Direct Effect database, select "Game," then "Direct Effects" from the main menu.

THE BASIC PAGE

The Basic page allows you to enter a name for your effect, as well as a note for personal reference. The "Type" is set on the Custom page.

THE CUSTOM PAGE

The Custom page allows you to set options such as the success rate of the effect, the possible targets for the effect, and how the effect acts in battle.

SETTINGS

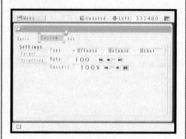

The Settings page allows you to set the Type, Rate, and Success percentage of the effect.

TYPE: Determines whether the effect is classified as "Offense," "Defense," or "Other." It also determines which in-game menu the effect is placed in.

RATE: Determines how effective the effect is.

SUCCESS: Controls the member's percentage chance of success. For example, placing "50" here means the effect is successfully executed 50 percent of the time.

TARGET

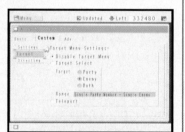

This page allows you to specify the target for your effect.

DISABLE TARGET MENU: Check this box if the effect applies only to the user or does not require a target.

TARGET SELECT: Determines if the effect can be used on the party, the enemy, or both. "Range" determines whether the effect can be used randomly between the party and an enemy unit.

TELEPORT: Check this box when creating a teleport effect. When selected in-game, the locations set within the Script Command "Party/Teleport/Set Teleport" appear.

DIRECTING

The Directing page allows you to determine how the effects act in battle.

GROUP: Select a Script Command within the "Group" field if the effect targets multiple party members or enemies.

SUCCESS: Call a Script Command within the "Success" field to display a visual effect when the effect is a success.

CRITICAL: Call something to be displayed on the occasion of a special success.

CUSTOM: A script called up here occurs when the condition set in "Adv/Result/Custom" is met.

FAIL: "Fail" is displayed if the user fails to execute the attack.

THE ADVANCED PAGE

The Advanced page deals with very specific and advanced options regarding battle flow that should only be altered by the most experienced users.

FLOW1

The first Flow page allows you to set exactly when the effect begins and ends.

TURN START: Scripts that deal with attack order are called up here. This occurs before any member or enemy starts their turn.

TURN END: These scripts are applied after the current turn ends.

CHECK START: This is the stage where the system verifies whether or not an effect can be used. For example, the Script Command "Start MP" checks to see whether the enemy or member has enough Magic Points to use the effect.

CHECK FAIL: If the check fails, a script such as "Ban Ability" disallows the effect.

EFFECT START: If the check succeeds, the effect occurs. For example, the "Cast Magic" Script Command allows magic to be cast.

COUNTERATTACK: If the effect causes a counter-attack, the counterattack script is called out here.

CONSUME: This deducts the cost of the effect from the appropriate pool. Select "Death Check Before" to have the system check for the death status before it deducts the cost of the effect.

FLOW2

This page is a continuation of the Flow1 page.

FIRST EFFECT: The rate of damage as it is applied to the first target the effect hits.

AFTER EFFECT: The rate of damage as it is applied to any additional targets the effect hits.

SUCCESS CHECK: Determines whether or not the effect is successful. A common Script Command within this field is "Magic Formula1."

NOTE

Use First Effect and Multi-Effect only if the rates are different between successive hits.

RESULT

The Result tab allows you to specify what occurs when an effect succeeds or fails.

SUCCESS: Here you set what occurs when an effect succeeds.

(CRITICAL): The content specified here occurs when a special hit is performed.

(CUSTOM): The content specified here occurs after the content specified in "Success" occurs.

FAIL: This content is applied if the success check fails.

DODGE: This occurs if the success check passes but the target dodges the effect.

INDIRECT EFFECTS

The Indirect Effect Database contains over 30 Indirect Effects that can be used as is, or altered to suit your preferences. Indirect Effects are effects that happen over time, such as Poison or Sleep.

THE BASIC PAGE

NAME: Enter a name for your effect in this field.

NOTE: Enter a note that is placed in the Indirect Effects Database.

TYPE: The type is set in the "Advanced" page under "Modify."

USABLE: Indirect Effects are usable in Battle, on the World Map, or both. Change where the effect is usable on the "Advanced" page under "Flow 2."

CUSTOM PAGE

The Custom page allows you to set the Indirect Effect's priority, duration, effectiveness, resistances, and so on.

SETTINGS

The Settings page allows you to enter text that will appear within the in-game Stat menu, choose a symbol to represent the effect, set a priority number, and set the effectiveness of the effect.

TEXT: What you enter here will be displayed within the in-game Stat menu when the Indirect Effect is applied.

SYMBOL: Symbol is displayed next to the afflicted character's name in the Who menu.

PRIORITY: Priority controls what occurs when multiple Indirect Effects of the same type are applied. The effect with the higher priority number will be applied. Refer to "Adv/Modify/Priority Match" to dictate how multiple Indirect Effects of the same priority number are handled.

RATE: Rate determines how effective the Indirect Effect is.

LENGTH

Set how long the Indirect Effect will last on this page.

STEPS: Set how many steps the character must take before the Indirect Effect wears off.

RATIO: Set the percentage chance the Indirect Effect will end per step.

BATTLE: "Targeted" refers to how many times a character is targeted (by friend or foe) before the effect wears off. Or, choose "Turns" and set how many times the entire party must takes a turn before the effect wears off.

TOTAL: The number entered here represents the total amount of "Turns" or "Targeted" actions must occur before the effect runs its course.

RATIO: Same as "Steps," but this field deals with the percentage chance the effect will dissipate per "Turn" or "Targeted."

RESIST W/RESIST M

These two pages allow you to set resistance to weapons and magic respectively.

WEAPON RESIST %: Set a weapon resistance here and then apply this Indirect Effect to an item in "Item Editor/Custom/Equipped/Indirect Effect." Once you equip that item, you will gain the resistances set here.

RESIST M: Same as weapon resistances, but equipping an item applied with this Indirect Effect will raise magic resistances, rather than weapon resistances.

ADVANCED PAGE

Allows you to set the type and status of the Indirect Effect, as well as determine how the effect is treated.

MODIFY

Select the type and status here, as well as how a priority match is handled.

TYPE: "Action" status means the afflicted character cannot perform any actions. "Condition" is any effect that raises or lowers attributes. "Magic" and "Skill" statuses disable the use of magic and skills by the character. "Custom" is any status not covered by the other four.

STATUS: If Condition, Magic, or Skill is set as the "Type," you can choose a status such as Poison or Blind.

PRIORITY MATCH: Determine what occurs if two effects of the same priority number hit the character. "Overwrite" means the most current effect overwrites the earlier effect. "Combine Rates" allow you to combine the rates of multiple effects up to a maximum percentage. "Combine: lengths" allow the durations of the effects to stack up to a certain percentage.

If "Action Status" is chosen as the type, you will get different menu selections.

INCAPACITATE: All actions will be disabled but the target will not be defeated. Sleep is an example of an incapacitation effect.

DEFEAT: Defeat will make the target unable to continue. Death is an example of a Defeat effect.

FLEE: If the battle is won, the afflicted character will recover from a Flee effect. However, if the entire party is similarly afflicted, the party dies. Check the "Enable Experience" box if you want a character to still receive experience if the battle is won while s/he is suffering from a Flee effect.

FLOW 1

Here you determine how the Indirect Effect is treated.

NEW SUCCESS: The script chosen within the "New Success" field occurs at the time the Indirect Effect is initially applied to the target.

COMBINED SUCCESS: This script is applied when two Indirect Effects are applied to the target.

FAIL: This script occurs when the Indirect Effect fails.

FORCED END: This occurs when the Indirect Effect is forcibly ended. For example, an antidote can forcible end a poison effect.

NATURAL END: This occurs when the effect runs its course naturally.

FAIL: This occurs when a cure attempt fails.

FLOW 2

You can set where an Indirect Effect is usable and when the effect is applied on this page.

USABLE: Select "Battle," "World," or "Both." If "Battle" is selected, the effect will end after battle. Select "Both" if you do not want the effect to end after a battle.

EACH RESULT: Select a script that applies the effect every time the afflicted character moves on the map.

TURN STAR: You can choose to apply content right before the entire battle turn begins by selecting a script within this field.

CHARACTER END: Applies an effect right after a character's turn ends.

TURN END: Applies an effect right after the entire turn has ended.

REFLECTED: A script called up within this field occurs when an ability or attack is reflected back on the instigator.

CHECK START: Occurs right before the check occurs to decide if the action will be performed.

AFTER RESULT: Occurs right after the Indirect Effect is applied.

INTRODUCTION

This is a world where people live peaceful lives and prosperity flourishes across the land.

As a young boy, your veins flow with energy and your heart pounds for adventure. Your parents, while not wealthy, manage to make ends meet with the help of the family business—a local inn, snuggled here in the secluded village of San Moreek.

You spend your days scampering around the rocky hills behind the village and often play pranks on local residents. Rarely are you seen without your partner in crime and childhood friend, Cocona. Your life is simple, if not a bit tedious.

One day…

While looking after the inn for your father, two shady men enter. You hesitantly give them a room for the night and soon forget about it until the royal kingdom soldiers show up seeking these men. This is a day you'll never forget.

The mysterious item left behind invites you on a wonderful journey and a life changing experience—one where a boy becomes a man….

WORLD MAP

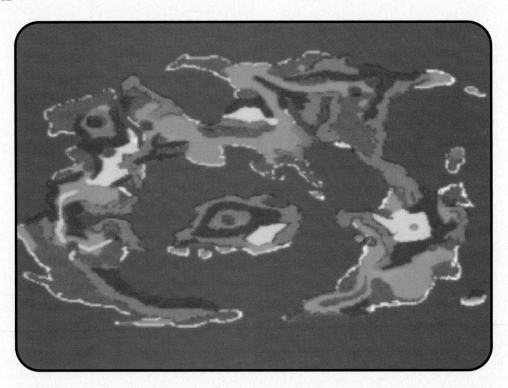

BASICS

This section covers all the basics that your party needs to maneuver through the vast world of fu-ma. Check this section carefully, because some of the information might save your life. Press ⇩ to bring up the in-game menu, which offers Talk, Item, Stats, Magic, Look, and Setup menus.

MOVEMENT
WALKING

Walking is easy in the world of fu-ma. Press any direction on the D-pad and your characters walk in that direction. You always walk at the same speed.

SAILING

Hooligan looks at the ocean...

Sailing comes later in the game, when you board a boat. Controls are the same as if you were walking—move up, down, left, or right by pressing on the D-pad. Use the menu to look at objects or use magic while you're on the boat.

TALK

Who are you talking to?

It is important to talk to people you find along your journey. Some of your conversations are idle chitchat, but some produce valuable information for your quest. Some people even give you items and objects. Try to talk with everyone. Sometimes you return later in your quest and talk to the same people for new information or objects.

Stand next to the person you want to talk to. From your in-game option menu, select "Talk" and your conversation begins. If you are not right next to the person you wish to converse with, you get the message "Who are you talking to?"

RESTING

Welcome to our inn. One night is 32G. Would you like to stay?

You rest at inns around the world of Fu-ma. As you get farther away from your hometown, the stays cost more and more. When you find an inn, go inside and talk to the person in the lobby. Agree to the price and you'll soon be refreshed and full of life and magic.

BUYING/SELLING

Welcome back! What can I do for you?

Buying and selling can be done at any of the shops or with any of the merchants scattered about the world of Fu-ma. Simply talk to a merchant to get the options to buy or sell items.

Select "Buy" to see the merchant's wares. Use the D-pad to scroll through the list. Press to the right if you want to increase the quantity of the item you wish to purchase. Press ✗ to confirm the sale, then select who you want to carry the object.

Select "Sell Item" to view your own stash. Use the D-pad to choose the items you want to sell. Scroll down the list and press ✗ when you find an item to sell. If the price from the merchant is agreeable, select "Yes."

ITEMS

Items are objects in the game, ranging from weapons to keys. Press ⇩ to bring up your in-game menu and choose "Item." This menu shows you all the items that each character has.

You can choose to "Use," "Give," "Equip," "Destroy," or "End" a character's items. Some items from your inventory can be used, such as Mushrooms and Feathers. Other items can be used during encounters, such as the Sunfire Staff during attacks.

EQUIPPING

Weapons and armor must be equipped before they can be used. Select the weapon or armor you want, then select "Equip." When an item is equipped, it is marked with an "E" in the item menu.

BAG

You receive the bag in the beginning of the game. Use it to store extra items you don't want your party to carry. You can access the bag's items as if a character was carrying them. Duplicate items stack up to save room.

STATS

Select this option to view the statistics for each of your characters. You can view their level, what they have equipped, how much experience they have, and also their maximum health and magic.

MAGIC

Go to the "Magic" option to view each character's available spells. When not in battle, you can use the spells to help your party. Some helpful spells could heal a party member, help you escape from a dungeon, or teleport you to a town you've already visited.

LOOK

Sometimes during your travel you find interesting

things on the ground. Step next to the object and choose "Look" to get it. If the object is just part of the scenery, you get the message "There is nothing special here."

INSPECTING

You need to inspect some items to find hidden objects. Objects that can hold collectable items are treasure boxes, vases, barrels, and cupboards.

SAVING/LOADING

To save your game, visit a church or holy site in one of the towns. Once inside, find a red book on a pedestal in one of the corners. Select "Look" to examine the book and you get the option to record your journey. If you have a memory card, select "Yes." Then select the memory card slot, and where you want to

put your saved game. If you choose not to record your progress, you can exit your journey altogether.

READING

Many towns in your adventure offer important reading material. Look at a bookshelf to get the option to read. Select "Yes" and fill your head with valuable knowledge.

SETUP

This option lets you adjust game play. You can equip your characters, change the order of your party, change the text speed, turn on vibration, or adjust the audio.

ENCOUNTERS

Encounters are a necessary occurrence in the world of fu-ma. Most of the time you don't have to find trouble—it finds you. As soon as you leave the safety of a village or castle, you're fair game for any enemy creeping about the area.

But by fighting you gain experience, gold, and maybe even a treasure box with goodies inside. You might prefer the path of peace, but the monsters leave you little choice. Defeat them in battle and enjoy the fruits of your victory!

It might seem like a nice day for a walk…

…until you stumble across unseen enemies and start an encounter. These enemies are all over the world. You won't even see them first.

As long as you've entered the encounter, you must make a few decisions. You can either fight or flee. The setup feature allows you only to manipulate the speed of the text you read and auto-fights the battle for you.

BASIC FIGHTING STRATEGIES

Selecting which enemy you want to attack is important. If only one enemy is attacking, your choice is easy. If there are more than one, consider your options.

The more numerous your enemies, the greater your chance of taking damage. Try to thin out the opposition. Focus your team's attention on one enemy at a time and try to defeat that enemy before it can get a shot off.

NOTE

It is safe to have all your group members attack the same enemy. Once the targeted enemy is defeated, the party members who haven't attacked yet start fighting the next opponent in line.

As you play, learn your opponents' strengths and weaknesses. If any enemy doesn't have a very powerful attack, conserve your magic points and just use a normal attack.

If you run into some really powerful enemies, unleash your arsenal on them before they get you. Try to take out the most dangerous enemy first.

FIGHT

If you choose to fight, gold and experience await you if you win. You might even find a treasure box left behind. But don't die, or you won't get any of it. After you select the "Fight" option, you get six sub-options: "Attack," "Magic," "Defend," "Skill," "Item," and "Equip."

ATTACK

Familiarize yourself with this option, because you use it a lot. After you choose this option, you get to select which enemy you want to hit first. Press up or down on the D-pad to select, then press ✕.

Select how and who your first party member will attack, then repeat the process for the other characters in your party.

Your characters attack the enemy, and you see how much damage you inflicted. If you hit your enemy for more damage points than it has health points, you defeat the enemy and it disappears.

If you didn't hit the enemy for enough points—or there is another enemy—the battle is still on. Select "Fight" again, then "Attack," then select the enemy you want to hit.

When your enemies have all been defeated, you win! You receive experience points and gold. On special occasions, you also receive a treasure box.

MAGIC

If your character has better spells than attack power, choose the magic option. Spells come in three categories: "Offense" for attack, "Defense" to help you or your team, and "Other," which comprises non-combat spells.

Your offensive spells work like the attack option. After you choose "Offense," select the spell you want to use, then the enemy you want to use it against.

Defensive spells and other spells work basically the same way. Defensive spells can only be used on members of your own team; the "Other" category includes spells that can be used on both bad and good guys.

DEFEND

If someone in your group has been taking a pounding, the "Defend" option might be the solution. When you select this, you forfeit an attack, but you don't take as much damage, and you can let those with more health points do the fighting.

SKILL

When you want to try out a player's particular skill, choose this option.

ITEM

Choosing this option lets you use an item that a character is holding. Items are particularly useful when, for example, a player who is low on magic power has an item that produces the same effect.

Caution

Make sure that the item you want to use is on the character, not in the bag. If it's not on the character, you can't use it.

EQUIP

This option ensures that your armor and weapons are equipped for battle.

FLEE

"Flee" is a great option if you've been hammered in battle and can't afford to fight anyone, or if the fighting is a bit tedious. Use the D-pad to select this option and press ✕.

Sometimes it works well, and you're gone like the wind.

Other times it fails, and you're stuck fighting. But all is not lost. Fight through one round, and when the "Flee" option is presented again, go for it. It might work the second time.

San Moreek

After you choose your hero's name, the game begins. You start in your family's inn, where Prime Minister Ramzie is sleeping peacefully. Bilton leaves you in charge to watch the inn and keep it quiet.

Unfortunately, Ramzie doesn't sleep long. Your mother, Anessa, comes yelling down the stairs. She needs you to pick 20 Mushrooms for dinner. She even gives you a bag to put them in. After the prime minister leaves, you can get on your way.

TIP

Whenever you enter a new building or area, check for hidden items. Wooden cupboards, vases, barrels, treasure boxes, and bookcases can all have secret treasures for you to use or interact with.

NOTE

Because this is an inn, you can always come back to rest and replenish your health. And because it's family-owned, it's free! Just go upstairs and stand next to the bed to get the option to rest.

After you get the Health Mushroom and Leather Shield from the inn, exit out the back door and run into the nearby shack.

Push the wooden block out of the way to get into the treasure box. Return to the city after you grab the Clover Charm and chat with the villagers to see what news they might have.

A few goodies are scattered about the town. Check the building south of the inn for a Cure Mushroom and the house to the west of the inn for a Leather Hat. These are some good items to have before you go out for Mushrooms.

When you're ready to get the Mushrooms, run up the small hill in the back of the town and follow the dirt path to the right of the church. Check your items and make sure you are fully equipped and ready for battle. When you're ready, follow the dirt path to the Mushroom Hill.

You find Cocona, and she wants to help you pick the Mushrooms. That's good, because you need the help. Climb the ladder or explore the bottom floor to find the Mushrooms. When you find one, walk up to it and choose the option to look at it. Then you can collect it.

ENCOUNTERS

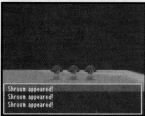

Hungry Snake

Ooze

Vampire Bat

Shroom

All these enemies are lower-level creatures, but they can do some serious damage to you because you are just starting the game. Your hero is strong enough to take out the Vampire Bat and the Shroom with a single swipe from his weapon. The Hungry Snake and Ooze are a little stronger and may take two turns to destroy.

Lucky for you, Cocona has a powerful Fire spell that quickly kills any of these creatures. If possible, have your hero attack what you know he can kill during the first round.

NOTE

Collecting Mushrooms and fighting monsters is hard work. If you run low on health points or magic points, leave the area and visit the inn to get recharged.

TIP

Even though you are supposed to collect the Mushrooms for your mom, you can use some yourself. If you get injured, use one to replenish your health. It only gives you a little health, but every bit helps when you're almost dead.

18, 19, 20! When you have at least 20 Mushrooms, return to your mom and leave the monsters on the hill behind you.

Your mother is glad to see you have the Mushrooms for her. For your good deeds, Cocona leaves your party and you have to help your father run the inn.

Watching the inn is more exciting than you thought. When the soldiers chase the thieves, run outside after them. When the excitement is over, enter the inn again. Talk to your family. It looks like the thieves left behind an old vase. It might be stolen from the castle. You'd better take it back.

TIP

Save your game as often as you can. Visit the church and look at the little red book in the corner. It gives you the option to save your progress. The church is also a great place to visit if a party member dies or gets sick.

Before you venture out into the dangerous world, properly equip yourself. Make a run for the shop and purchase anything you think you might need for your journey. If you explored the area, you don't need any armor. And if you picked and pocketed some extra Mushrooms earlier, you don't need any Health Mushrooms.

The castle is only a quick walk away. After you exit your village, head to the right and follow the yellow trail. You might fight a few enemies along the way, but it's nothing you can't handle.

ENCOUNTERS

Blood Bee

Blood Bees like to travel around with the same creatures you saw on Mushroom Hill. They're not too difficult to destroy. A hit from your hero should do the trick. Remember that you only have your hero to fight with, so at most you can only kill one opponent per round.

SANKEREST CASTLE

There's the castle in all its glory. Walk in to find the king.

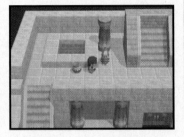

Cross the bridge over the moat and enter the castle. Go up the short stairs on either side in the back of the room. One more set of stairs on the second level leads to an audience with the king.

THE CAT'S MEOW

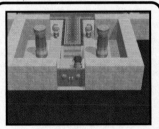

Before you talk to the king, take a little breather outside. Go around the stairs you just ascended and head through the double doors to the top of the castle.

THE CAT'S MEOW CONTINUED

The people up there have interesting stories, but it's the cat you really want to talk to. It's the one with the red choker. It meows *two* times at you. Remember that for later.

Now back to the business at hand. Go back inside and chat with the king. He's the guy in the big chair wearing the funny red hat. It turns out the vase didn't come from the castle after all. Those thieves must have stolen it from somewhere else. But where?

The king's daughter is in the corner with an ugly Dragon Doll on the table. Maybe you'll get a chance to get it from her later.

Before you leave the castle, check the cupboards in the back right corner. This is royalty and they should have some good stuff for you to…borrow. A Bird Feather and Health Mushroom should come in handy.

So the vase didn't come from the castle. Maybe your parents would have a clue as to where to go next. When you get back to the inn and talk to Bilton he informs you that Cocona is upstairs with your mother.

Talk to your mom upstairs. She wants you to store the vase in the barn out back. On your way, you bump into Cocona's grandpa. He thinks the vase was stolen from the Grand Shrine. Maybe the priest in Prahidel has some answers.

You won't be going on this journey alone. Cocona joins you, with her grandfather's blessings. Head for the shop in town and buy Cocona a Leather Shield and a Leather Hat. Now leave San Moreek and head for the castle, but don't enter it. Instead, follow the yellow path on the opposite side as it leads north.

ENCOUNTERS

Baby Dragon

Slasher

The enemies around this part can be deadly, and the Baby Dragon is the most dangerous. Use Cocona's Fire spell on it while your hero supports her with his attack. After disposing of the Baby Dragon, move on to any other monsters trying to hurt you. Left to its own devices, the Baby Dragon tries to roast everybody in your party.

The archway spanning the path is where you want to go. Walk into it to enter the guard station.

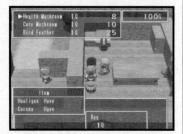

Inside the guardhouse, you find a traveling merchant in the side room. Talk to him if you need more supplies.

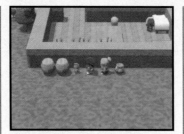

Walk through the guard station, but don't follow the yellow path into the dark green area yet. When the path stops, make a right. Follow the line of trees and make a right turn after the last one. Look at the Robot Doll on the ground to acquire it. Now head into the dark green grass to continue your journey.

Continue to follow the yellow path. When it ends, cross the small patch of green grass and enter a large sandy area. Continue to move in a northeasterly direction. Climb up a dirt ramp when you see it. Keep heading northeast as you follow the dirt trail.

ENCOUNTER

Goblin

Buzzard

Goblins are tricky critters. Not only do they like to hack and slash you, but they also can cast spells to weaken your defenses. Buzzards like to peck you apart. It takes the combined powers of both your characters to take down one of these creatures. If Cocona is strong enough, she might be able to help your hero by just attacking and not wasting her magic.

PRAHIDEL

When you get to the end of the dirt trail, you can see Prahidel a little way ahead. Time to get rest at the inn.

The two thieves who left the vase at your inn are here. After they argue for a bit, they leave to find their next target. No use worrying about them now—you're on a mission.

The inn is to your right. Stop on by and take a rest to replenish your health and magic. While you're there, look in some of the vases and cupboards upstairs and downstairs to find a Health Mushroom and some gold.

When your health is fully replenished, visit the church in the center of town to save your game. Check the barrels around the church for a hidden Health Mushroom and…why is there a Robot Doll on the roof? You can't reach for it yet, so move on, but don't forget about it.

The mayor's house is behind the church. He knows where the Shinto priest is. He tells you that the priest Loian went to the North Cemetery. Talk to the ghost somewhere in the house to learn more about the old city that used to be there.

After you exit the house, head left and enter a second door that leads inside. Check the vases and cupboards for some items such as a Bird Feather, Clothed Armor, and gold as you make your way up the stairs. On the top floor, talk to the ghost of the Ancestor.

Exit the mayor's house and go around back to talk to the boy about his missing dog, Po-Chi. Make your way to the shop to the right of the mayor's house. Before you talk to the shop owner, loot the place of a Health Mushroom and a Leather Hat. With goods in hand, enter the shop from the front and stock up on any supplies you might need.

You haven't yet ransacked another shop close to the entrance. Before you go in the front door, make your way through the back door and get a dagger out of the treasure box behind the shop owner. Don't worry; they won't miss it.

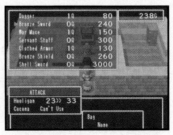

Go around and enter through the normal entrance. It's time to upgrade your weapon. The Bronze Sword is just what your hero needs to fight off enemies at the old cemetery where Loian is.

After you exit Prahidel, journey to the north and follow a thin green path west through the forest. Walk into the cross to enter the North Cemetery.

Walk to the top of the cemetery and you find Loian praying. It's not long before Po-Chi runs into a dangerous area, causing Loian to fall into a hole. Run to the edge of the hole and you hear that Loian needs help. You better go back to town and talk to the mayor.

Back in the city, go talk to the mayor in his big house. He's not happy to hear of Loian's fate. He says he will look for the key and catch up to you at the North Cemetery. Get going!

When you get back to the cemetery, go to the door on the left instead of up the stairs. The mayor arrives with the key and unlocks the door for you. Too bad his back hurts, or he'd help you. Yeah, right! Go inside to start the rescue without him.

You don't have to go far to find Po-Chi and Loian. Unfortunately, they're trapped inside a room. You have to find some way to get inside to help them.

Encounters

Skull

Beholder

Zombie

Encounters Continued

Underneath the city are plenty of scary monsters to keep you company. Watch out for the Skulls, which have a mean bite and can even cast spells. The Zombie is a tough customer who can do a lot of damage and can even poison one of your characters. The Beholder is no slouch and can cast an attack spell for some significant damage.

In battle, try to take out the Zombies and Skulls first because they do the most damage in the long run.

Follow the wide yellow path to the right of Loian and Po-Chi. Before you follow the path up the dirt ramp at the end, make a left past the well. Go around the crumbling walls until you can enter the room and inspect all the vases and the treasure box. A Cure Mushroom and Wooden Doll fit nicely in your bag.

Now return to the large yellow path and go up the dirt path. Follow this dirt path to the right and climb the stairs.

The upstairs looks nicer than that dirty cave. Follow the stonework to the left. Keep following it left until you can head north and descend a flight of stairs. Get the Servant Staff from the treasure box below, then return upstairs.

Back upstairs, head to the right but keep to the south path. You come to a small area with two black holes in the ground. Walk into the left one to fall into the darkness below.

That was a nice fall. You landed in the room with Loian and Po-Chi. After you move the rubble away from the door, follow Loian back to the mayor's house.

Back at the mayor's house, you learn a little about the vase, which you are advised to show to the Great Shinto Priest at the Grand Shrine. Loian will go with you.

Before you leave, visit the inn to replenish your health and magic. Visit the shops to get needed items, such as a War Mace for Loian. And, finally, visit the church to save your progress so far.

It's time for a long journey. Consult the World Map in this guide if you get lost. Once you leave Prahidel, head east, following the light green grass.

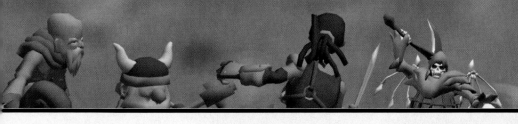

Encounters

Imp

Rabid Flower

Imps are dangerous creatures. Not only do their attacks cause a lot of damage, but they also have a devastating spell to confuse your characters. Have Cocona cast Harmony to block their spells before they have a chance to use them, then beat them down with your normal attacks. If a Rabid Flower is nearby, finish off your enemy as quickly as possible because Rabid Flowers like to heal their fighting partners.

If you follow the green grass east, you eventually run into a small inn. If it was a long hard journey, you can rest to heal your wounds.

Inside, talk to the people to learn about a mysterious cave nearby, as well as the Grand Shrine. A man inside is selling wares if you need to buy anything. Some Ornate Armor for Cocona would be a good idea. Don't forget to check the cupboards for a Health Mushroom.

Outside the inn, follow the grass path north. When the ocean blocks your path north, head to the right. Follow the coast as you move through the forest. Soon you get to a clearing with a strange object on a wooden stump. Look at it and you get a Wooden Doll!

Return to the edge of the forest you just came from. To the south of your position, a green path heads east. Get on it and start walking.

GRAND SHRINE

After a long hard march, you've finally made it. That ancient-looking building is the Grand Shrine, and inside is the Great Shinto Priest you need to talk to.

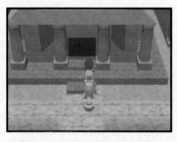

Three buildings make up the Grand Shrine. Enter the largest one in the center to save your progress in the journal book. The book is in the top right corner of the room. A large door in the back of the room is too heavy for you to open.

After you talk to the citizens and save your game, exit the building and head to the building to the left. Check the cupboards in each of the rooms for Clothes and a Wooden Club. After you collect your things and chat with everybody, you can leave.

You have one more building to explore. Head to the far right and enter that building. The Great Shinto Priest must be there.

As you walk down the center hall, inspect the side rooms. The cupboards have a Sentry Helm and the bookshelves have interesting reading material.

At the end of the hall, you finally meet the Great Shinto Priest, who has some interesting news for you. The vase you have is the Vase of the Seal. It's the vase that imprisoned Jadece, the King of the Demons!

With the vase no longer in your possession, you might think your problems are over. Think again. You have to find the three Tears of Power to renew the seal! Oh, well. Time to put your butt on the line helping others again.

Encounters

Werewolf

Raptor

These creatures pack quite a punch. They don't have any magical power, but they are physically powerful and they like to strike before you. If you encounter a group of three or four enemies, don't hesitate to use Cocona's Blast to strike all the opponents. It might be the only thing to save your life.

From the Grand Shrine, your path leads south. Follow the light green path down to the ocean. By then, you should see a palm tree on a sandy beach. Walk into it to see what's going on there.

Some evil monsters are tormenting a turtle. Luckily, Loian is able to bore them with his preaching. Eventually they fall asleep and you can chat with the turtle. He tells you that there is something shiny in the ocean east of San Moreek. Maybe if you get a boat you can check it out.

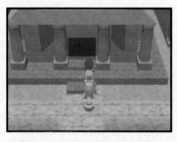

The turtle is safe, so you can leave. Follow the green path to the right and up the dirt slope into the mountains. This mountain range goes north and south; your destination for now is to the south.

Eventually the mountain range ends and you can descend a dirt slope and enter a forested area. Follow the path until you enter the yellow sandy area. Move south until you can climb another slope into another set of mountains.

Encounters

Rock Bear

Ogre

These creatures have a lot of hit points and can hit you for a lot of damage. Try to concentrate all your attacks on a single enemy, because it takes everything you have to bring down one of these guys, especially a Rock Bear.

Follow this new dirt trail to the south. When you come to the open green patch, work your way north.

SEAPOOL

That large city next to the dock must be Seapool. It's a hotspot for sailors. Maybe you can get a boat there to scout the ocean for treasure. At the very least, it should have an inn to rest your weary bones.

After you enter the city, walk up the stone ramp and follow the gray walkway as it winds left. A few people you see along the way tell you there's a commotion near the docks.

When you start to descend the stone ramp, you can tell that something is going on. Talk to the guys wearing blue hats on the dock and you learn that those two thieves are at it again. They are trying to steal the old ship docked there. Too bad it's a wreck and will probably sink on them.

The docks are a busy place with curious onlookers. Fight your way through them and head to the north until you see a man guarding a door. That's the ship repair port.

Go through the door to a huge warehouse. Check the barrel for a Health Mushroom first. Go to the dock and chat with Shuban. After you agree to join his crew, he runs off for lunch. Follow him outside.

The Cat's Meow

Once you get back outside, walk to the right and look at some barrels to find a Magic Mushroom. Near the barrels is a mangy gray cat with a yellow choker. Talk to it and it meows *seven* times.

Walk around the raised area until you come to a small house on the lower level. Shuban and his brother, Raban, are arguing inside. Raban doesn't want his brother to become a pirate. Shuban says he won't if Raban goes to the Tower of Flame and brings back the Pirate King Hat.

When you talk to Raban again he tells you to get out, but he changes his tone when he realizes you can help him. He says if you'll let him join your party, he'll give you whatever you want. Agreed! After he joins your group, return to the city.

NOTE

Raban is only a temporary member of your group. You can't equip him with any armor, weapons, or items. During a fight he automatically attacks the leftmost enemy on the screen. Sometimes he attacks with his melee weapon, but other times he casts a spell for extra damage.

Walk up the stone ramp and enter the church to the north. Record your data here before heading back out into the wild.

The inn is to the south of the church. Go inside and rest to refill your stats. When you go back outside, talk to the clown. He has an expensive doll for sale. You can't buy it just yet, but come back when you have the money.

By this point in your journey you probably need to upgrade your armor and weapons. Lucky for you, there are two shops in town. Be sure to get the Holy Blade for your hero and the Talisman for both Cocona and Loian. If you can, upgrade all your weapons and armor except for the Leather Hat your hero has. You find a nice helm for him in a bit.

Save one more time, then find that Pirate King Hat for Raban. Exit Seapool and head south. Let the coastline be your guide. It won't be long before the tall gray Tower of Flame stands before you.

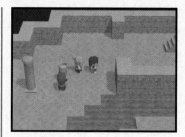

Enter the tower and walk through the double doors. Walk around the water to the left and follow it north. Climb the set of stairs you eventually come to.

Encounters

Tower Golem

Mutant Fly

Griffon

The Mutant Flies aren't that bad, but they usually come along with tough creatures. The Tower Golem is an extremely rugged beast. Magic works better against it than traditional melee weapons. Try as you might, you probably won't defeat it after the first round, even with everyone attacking it. By the second round it should be nothing more than rubble.

Encounters Continued

The Griffon is a horrible foe. It can take half of your life with one swift hit. Luckily, it attacks alone so you can concentrate all your firepower on it. Hopefully, it gets only one or two shots on your party before it dies.

When you get to the second floor, inspect the treasure boxes for a Bronze Helm and a Moon Spear. That helm would look good on your hero, and Loian could use a new weapon.

NOTE

Some treasure boxes around the area seem out of reach…for now. You have to enter the tower from a different way to access certain areas. But that comes a little later.

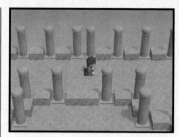

Climb the other set of stairs on the landing. When you get to the next landing, climb another set to a large room filled with stone columns. Why do you walk around them? To get to the other side, of course!

On the other side of the room are two treasure chests. One has a Sunbeam Staff, but the other has the hat you were looking for. Great! Now you can get out of this scary place. Equip Cocona with the staff and backtrack out of the tower. Make your way back north to Seapool.

TIP

The Sunbeam Staff that Cocona holds is a very powerful weapon. When in battle, select it as an item. It shoots a ball of flame at an enemy without using any magic points.

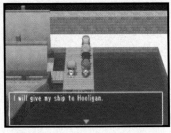

When you get back into town, return to the ship repair dock and talk with Shuban. He agrees to give up his pirate dreams because Raban returned with the Pirate King Hat. And since Shuban won't be a pirate, he won't need his pirate ship. Your party just gained a ship. Hurray!

Walk your crew onto the ship and it's bon voyage! Now you can sail the high seas. Should you become what the pirate Shuban wanted to be, and plunder and pillage the weak and the innocent? Sounds great! Oh, wait. You have a quest to complete first.

Once you're out on the ocean, head west until you see land. Follow the island around the south side while you continue to head west. Keep sailing past the wooden dock to the north.

Encounters

Horned Fish

Sea Dragon

Turtle Dragon

Starfish

The Horned Fish is a deadly sea creature that can inflict serious pain on a member of your party with a single blow. Don't let this happen. Use Cocona's Sunbeam Staff to wipe out this fish with one blow. If you're fighting more than one fish, take them out one at a time.

The Sea Dragon is another fierce enemy that can damage your whole party in a single swoop. Run if you can, but fight if you have to. Concentrate all your firepower on it. If it is traveling with a Mutant Fly, ignore the fly initially because it isn't as powerful as the dragon.

Encounters Continued

The Turtle Dragon is another deadly sea creature. Run if you can; it's not worth the energy to fight it. You always take a lot of damage. If you have to fight it, use a lot of powerful spells because melee weapons have little effect.

Starfish are more annoying than dangerous, especially when they travel in fours.

Soon you see a little island above you. To the left of the island, something sparkles in the water. Sail your ship over it and look. It's the Giant Hammer you heard about from the inn you visited earlier, and it's exactly where the turtle saw something shimmering in the ocean.

With hammer in hand, use your hero's Teleport spell to get back to Seapool. You end up in front of the city, and your ship is ready at the dock. Get a rest at the inn because you're about to start on a long journey.

Enter your boat and follow the coast south. When the land ends, follow the coast to the right. When you see the giant white cave, sail your ship on in.

Once inside, sail to the dirt floor and press ● to step off. Follow the dirt trail to a stone room. Climb the set of stairs you find.

Climb another set of stairs to another level. Walk around the water to get to a treasure box that contains some gold. Next walk through a small doorway near the stairs you just came up. Follow the hall as it winds to the right. I hope you're not tired, because you have to climb more stairs at the end.

Stick to the outer wall on the right and follow it as it goes down, to the left, then up. When it dead-ends, walk through the opening in the right wall. To the north is another set of stairs to climb.

Follow this new walkway to the right, through a doorway, then to the north. There's a closed door and somebody's passed out on the floor outside. It's a Shinto Priest who was out searching for the Tear of the Sun. He doesn't look so good. He expires, but not before giving you the World Map. Use it when you are traveling out in the open.

Before you go through the double doors, continue to follow the path. Open the treasure boxes at the end to get a Wooden Doll and a Sentry Shield. Now return to the double doors and go up the stairs.

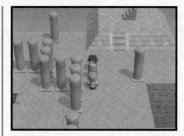

You emerge in a room surrounded by columns. In the center of the area is a raised platform with more stairs. Climb them and you get to another room with pillars. Walk either to the left or right past the pillars and climb the stairs in any corner of the room. They all lead to the same place.

When you get to the next room, you can see a raised area in the center. At the top, look at the pedestal and pick up the Tear of the Sun. One Tear down, two to go. Backtrack and exit the tower.

Once in your ship, set your sails to the west. You come to a little spit of land with a wooden dock. Exit the boat and enter the strange temple to the right.

Three small platforms surround a stone figure in the center. Look at each platform and place a Wooden Doll on each. After you place the third doll, the figure in the center becomes alive. Look at the figure to find out that its name is Dex, and it joins your group.

NOTE

Like Raban, Dex can't be equipped with any armor, weapons, or items. Dex automatically attacks the leftmost creature on your screen when you battle. Most of the time Dex attacks with his melee weapon, but occasionally he uses a spell that can damage multiple enemies in the same group.

With Dex in your group, you have more fighting power. Return to the boat and sail to the cave you explored earlier. This time, pass the cave instead of going in, and continue to sail east.

Follow the coast east, then north. When you see a dock, hit the shore again. On land, head north and climb the dirt ramp into the mountains. Follow the mountain trail as it continues north.

Encounters

Defiler

Moose

Both the Defiler and the Moose are bad company. The Defiler is strong and has a special attack that can leave a member of your party numb. The Moose is not only strong, but also tends to strike before the Defiler. Pool your strength to take out any Moose that gets in your way.

HEZAN

At the end of the mountain range, you see a small brown village nestled in the forest. That's the city of Hezan. Climb down from the mountain range and walk in the village to meet some more people on your journey.

Once you enter the city, make your way down the center road to the first house on the right. Check the cupboards inside for a Bronze Helm and the bookshelf for the Suncrest Map. The map tells of a hidden passageway behind the king's throne back at Sankerest Castle.

From this house go to the building across the street. Inside, you find a vase containing a valuable Magic Mushroom. These refill Cocona's magic power when she runs low.

Return to the street running down the center of town and follow it to a small well. Look into the well and your party climbs in. Move to the back corner and you find a Dragon Doll. When you're ready to leave, walk up to the rope and press up on the D-pad.

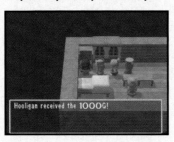

Once out of the well, head east up a small hill and into a little shack. The little old lady inside is sweet and invites you to make yourself at home. That's a great idea. Swipe her retirement nest egg of 1,000 gold, hidden in the cupboard. You might think that's all the money the old bag had, but check the barrel outside to find more of her gold for the taking.

Next to the little old lady's house is a gray brick wall and a set of stairs leading down. Only one way to find out where they lead: Follow them.

Below, it looks like a prison with three holding cells. Look at the bed in the center cell to get the Thief Key. With that key in your inventory, you can unlock the first cell and check the vase there for a Magic Mushroom.

The third cell holds a prisoner. Let him out if you want. All he was guilty of was trying to catch a glimpse of Granny's glorious body. At least that's what she says if you talk to her as she sits on the park bench outside.

Another small building is on the left, two buildings down from the jail. This is the church, in case you want to save your progress.

Hezan is a quaint little town, but it's time to leave. Exit the village and follow the mountain path back to your ship. Once on your ship you can continue your voyage north, following the coast.

Hug the coastline and you sail by a small island with a little cabin. You go there later, but for now keep sailing north. Eventually you hit another small island.

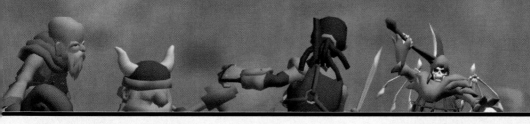

After you hit the small island, set sail to the west. Keep the coast of the main continent to your north as you sail. The big white cave is what you want to enter.

Land your boat and talk to another priest from the Grand Shrine. He's looking for the Tear of the Ocean, but can't get through the double doors because he needs the Coral Key to unlock them. You'd better find that key.

Before you search for the key, check the far dirt passage to the right. A treasure box with another Dragon Doll is at the end.

Encounters

Lizard Warrior

Frogkin

The Lizard Warrior carries a large sword and he knows how to use it. He can hit you for a lot of damage. Frogkin can do some damage, too. Kill them before they get a chance to cast anything against you. Given a choice, get the lizard first because he does the most damage.

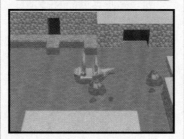

With your doll in hand, return to your ship and sail around the area where the priest is standing. In the back of the area are two entrances. You can sail into one; the other you have to walk into. For now, sail through the larger opening.

Jump on the dock and climb the ladder to a higher level. Go through the dark opening into the room beyond. There's nothing special here, so go through another dark doorway to the north.

Walk across the stone walkway and go through another doorway. Follow the corridor to a treasure box with a Water Ball inside. That comes in handy.

Return to the thin stone walkway you just crossed. On the other side, look at the large wheel. Do you want to steer it? You bet you do! The stone walkway lowers and the water rises. Backtrack to your boat.

On your boat again, sail into the blackness ahead. You enter a large cavern with three waterfalls and a black tunnel. Sail into the black tunnel.

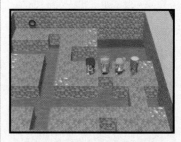

Sail to the right and set foot on land. Follow the path until you hit water, then make a left. Continue to follow the path until you get to a black circle in the wall. Look at it, then insert the Water Ball.

To the left of the circle, a waterfall stops flowing, revealing a dark passageway. It's big enough to sail your boat through. Jump back on board and get going.

Once you go through the dark entrance, follow the watery passageway. At the end you have a choice of three paths. Sail into the left tunnel; the other two just take you back to a cavern where you were before.

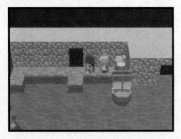

The left passage spits you back out near the beginning. There's only one way to go, so sail south back into the cavern with the priest. Go left and exit the boat to enter the doorway that's only accessible on foot.

Move through some rooms and climb some stairs. At the top, follow the passage right, over a stone walkway, and through another doorway. A treasure box awaits you, and the Coral Key is inside.

With Coral Key in hand, return to the double doors that priest was standing next to. Through the doors, you find two Squids blocking a doorway. Refill your health and prepare your supplies before you talk to them because you are in for a battle.

Encounters

Squid

Blood Squid

Both of these creatures are powerful and can knock off a large chunk of health with a single swipe. It's good if they only attack one member of your party at a time, because the Squid's powerful attack can damage the whole group. Concentrate all your power on the Squid first. Once he's dead, you are closer to winning the battle.

When both Squids are gone, walk through the door they were guarding. Inspect both treasure boxes to get a Circlet and the Tear of the Ocean. Two Tears down, one to go.

Return to your craft and exit the cave. Sail east and follow the coast of the continent. When you go around the continent, land is to the south. Head west.

Along your journey you pass another white cave. Ignore it for now and continue sailing to the right. Before you explore, you have to hit the last main city on the continent.

From the cave, sail southwest. Check your map if you need help. Finally you get to a small pier. Time to leave your ship again for a while and travel on dry land. From the pier, head east into the woods.

VILLAGE OF AGES

In a small circular valley surrounded by high mountains is the Village of Ages. This is the last city on the continent that you haven't visited. Walk inside, rest at the inn, and answer any questions you might have.

This village is built on a hill, so it has many levels. Walk up the ramp on the right to get to the second level. The first entrance you find is for the inn. Go inside and get some rest.

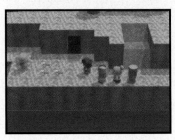

After you exit the inn, follow the pathway to the left through a dark tunnel. Next to a ramp leading to a higher level is a room you can enter.

Inside, check the cupboards for a Star Spear and the treasure box for a Dragon Doll. Talk with the shop clerk to buy some armor and weapons for your hero. Skip the Scale Armor, because you get some better armor soon enough.

Leave the shop and follow the path to the left. Soon you come to another dark door. Inside is another shop owner.

Leave this shop and walk down the ramp to the left. At the end of the trail, a man guards the Sacred Shrine. He won't let you in just yet. If you get in good with the village elder, he might change his mind.

Backtrack to the inn you rested in earlier. Walk around the corner to the right and stay on the second level. When the path ends, go into the dark doorway. Check the cupboards inside for some gold before you leave.

Around the corner from the room you just exited is a dirt ramp leading to the third level. Once you go up, head into the room on the left to visit a church and save your progress.

Leave the church and continue to walk around the area to the left. On the back of the hillside on the same level is another room. Check the cupboard for a Magic Apron.

The Cat's Meow

Inside is a cat with a blue choker. It meows *zero* times. That is the third cat you've seen on your journey with a colored choker.

Hooligan received the Fruit of Ages!

In the corner of the attached room, you find a set of stairs you can use to go downstairs. Check the cupboard for a Rabbit Foot, then talk to the man down there to get the Fruit of Ages. You can only have one at a time, so don't get greedy and ask for another one.

Climb the stairs and exit the room. Outside, keep going left, cross a small bridge, and climb another dirt ramp to reach the fourth level.

The Tear of Mother Earth is
safely stored in the Sacred
Cave here, locked away

The one room at the top is home
to the village elder. Talk to him to
find out how to get the Tear of
Mother Earth. It turns out that the
Tear is here, but it is locked
away. The key to get in was split
in two.

He is somewhere out there
in the world, protecting that
half of the key.

Half of the key is here in town;
the other was entrusted to a
village man's care. The man left
the village and is somewhere out
there in the world. Where could
he have gone? Maybe to the busy
port city of Seapool, where every
traveler seems to end up? Or
maybe he sought sanctuary
behind the sturdy walls of
Sankerest Castle? Or maybe he
moved to your home town of San
Moreek and was right under your
nose the whole time?

No matter where that villager
went, it's your job to find him. Exit
the village and board your sailing
vessel. Set sail to the east as you
follow the coast. It's time to visit
that cave you sailed past on your
way to the Village of Ages.

Sail past the cave, keeping the
coast to the south. Hit the first
pier you find and walk into the
lush green forest. Cut your own
trail to the west in search of that
white cave. Keep the coast above
you and you shouldn't have a
problem finding it.

Enter the cave and walk to the
right. To the north, some stairs
lead down to nothing, a big black
crack cuts the room in two. If you
try to walk over the crack, you
fall to the floor below and have to
climb the north stairs to get out.

Sweet! Silver Armor was found!

Giants must have been here. It's
time to get in the mood and grow
large. Have your hero check his
items and use the Giant Hammer.
Now you're big enough to step
over the crack without falling in.
Look at the large treasure box to
get the Silver Armor, then go
down the giant set of stairs.

Sweet! Phoenix Feather was found!

From the bottom of the stairs, go
right. Follow the path as it leads
north, but you soon come back
and cross those cracks. The trail
leads you to a treasure box
containing a Phoenix Feather.

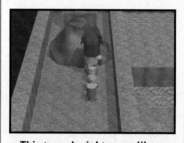

This tunnel might seem like a
dead end, but with your new girth
and size you can break stone.
Walk into the boulders to the
north of the treasure box and they
disappear, leaving a wide path
for your party to follow.

Sweet! Robot Doll was found!

The short trail leads to a large
treasure box with a Robot Doll.
Soon you'll have the whole set!
Now backtrack to those cracks
in the ground you skipped earlier.

There are three cracks in the
ground. Use the Giant Hammer
again to make yourself small, and
fall in the crack blocking the way
to the giant stairs leading down.

Your fall lands you in a lower
level next to a treasure box
containing 3,000 gold. Grab the
loot, walk off the ledge, and
climb the stairs out.

The treasure box is empty.

Time to use the hammer again to
grow large. Cross the crack and
descend the large stairs. Check
the large treasure box and you
get…nothing. It's empty. You're
so mad you could knock over a
bookshelf!

Move your huge form to the side of the bookshelf and push yourself into it. It slides out of the way, revealing a hidden area. Walk inside to find a treasure box with the Broken Key. You should have known that the villager with the second half of the broken key would've come here to the giant cave.

When you have the key, there's nothing left for you here. Take the magic option and cast Escape to leave the cave. Once outside, cast Teleport and select Village of Ages to return to the village elder.

Go to the top of the village and enter the room to talk to the village elder. He gives you the other half of the key to form the Ages' Key.

Now hightail it to the bottom level and the Sacred Cave, where the Shinto Priest was guarding the way. This time he lets you in. Look at the treasure box and you gain the Earth Tear.

RETURN TO THE GRAND SHRINE

Now that you have all three Tears, return to the Grand Shrine and talk with the Great Shinto Priest. Use the Teleport spell to get there in a hurry. Enter the building where you can deliver the three Tears.

Talk to the Great Shinto Priest and tell him that you have the Tears. Follow him to the center chapel. The worshippers there have been cleared out for the ceremony.

Once inside the chapel, go through the double doors in the back that were closed to you earlier. The priest is waiting for you.

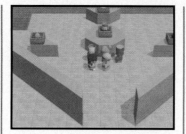

To start the ceremony, place the Tears on the stands. Just go up to a stand and look at it to place a Tear. After you place the third Tear, talk with the Shinto Priest again.

The ceremony starts as planned and the three Tears form into the Sacred Tear. But before the Sacred Tear can be placed on top of the Vase of the Seal, a creature named Liavo appears and steals the Vase.

That's messed up! At least the Sacred Tear isn't harmed. Follow the Shinto Priest back to his room, where he tells you to visit the sage who long ago fought the King of the Demons. First you deliver the Tears and know you have to find some old sage. When do you get to start living the pirate lifestyle?

Exit the Grand Shrine and teleport to the town of Hezan. Enter Hezan and climb the hillside to the right. Enter the little house and talk to the old man inside. He gives you the Sage's Key.

Exit Hezan and walk north. Cross a small bridge and you see a small building on a tiny island.

Walk into the building to see the sage's house and yard. Since you have the Sage's Key, walk through the door.

Inside, look at the left and right bookshelves for some interesting reading. Push the center bookshelf to the side and take a gander at it to find the sage's diary. He tells of the Bracelet of Light to defeat the King of the Demons. When you finish reading it, the door behind the bookshelf opens.

Take your party upstairs and look on the bed to pick up another Robot Doll. Look inside the treasure box for a Sacred Hood and the cupboard for a Gemstone Ring. Read the books for information about the three kinds of dolls.

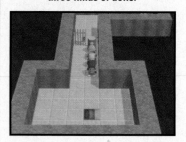

Exit down the stairs to the first floor of the sage's house, then take another flight of stairs down to the basement. Follow the passageway to another set of stairs leading down.

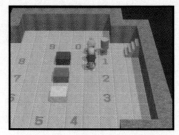

Down there you find 10 numbers on the floor, ranging from 0 to 9. The numbers form a ring, and in the center are red, blue, and yellow blocks. If the colors sound familiar, it's because they were the colors of the chokers you saw on some cats.

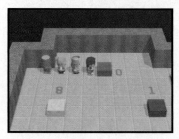

The cat with the yellow choker meowed seven times, so move the yellow block to the number 7. The cat with the red choker meowed two times, so the red block goes on the 2. The cat with the blue choker didn't meow at all, so move the blue block to the 0.

NOTE

Once you push a block on a number, it can't be moved again. But if you accidentally push a block on the wrong number, don't despair. Climb the stairs to exit the room and then re-enter. All the blocks will be reset in the center of the room.

When the blocks are in the correct place, Seramus appears and presents you with a treasure box containing the Bracelet of Light.

When you exit the house, you can see that the sky has grown dark. Could it be a sign of the return of the King of the Demons?

The evil Jadece has returned. His evil red eyes glow in delight that he has covered the world in darkness. He even has a surprise for the Grand Shrine.

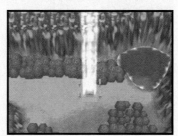

An evil magic leaves his palace and rains down on the Grand Shrine. What could it be? You'd better check it out.

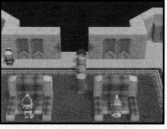

Before you go there, teleport to Sankerest and visit the king's throne room. Look at the diamond pattern on the back wall, and a secret passage opens.

Walk down the stairs to your left. Go through the doors in the next room and check out the treasure boxes for a Robot Doll and Bread.

Go down another flight of stairs and follow the brown passageway. When it forks, take the left trail and look at the vases at the end for a Health Mushroom.

Return to the fork and take the other path. Climb the stairs you find at the end to emerge outside of the castle. Go around the wall, cross the bridge, and leave the area.

Now use the Teleport spell again to go to the town of Prahidel. Walk to the center of town, where the church is located. On the left side of the roof is the Robot Doll you saw the first time you were here. Use the Giant Hammer to grow to a bigger size.

Once you're tall enough, get that doll. Walk over to the edge of the building and look at it to bring it into your inventory.

Leave the safety of the city and enter the wilderness. Walk east, keeping the mountain range to your north. Past the mountains, you see the ocean with your boat above you, then more mountains.

After a short walk, still keeping the second range of mountains to your north, you come to a break that you can cross over. There you find the Robot Temple in a little sandy alcove.

This temple is just like the one you visited for the woodman. Look at each platform to put down a Robot Doll. After you place the fifth doll, the Robot figure on the high center platform comes to life.

Climb the platform and look at the figure to hear what it has to say. Its name is Bulgil and it wants to join your group. Since you already have four members in your group, you have to say good-bye to Dex. Answer "Yes" to say good-bye, and you upgrade your party. Bulgil has joined the group!

NOTE

Like Dex, Bulgil can't be equipped with any armor, weapons, or items and always automatically attacks the leftmost creature on your screen in battle. Most of the time he attacks with his melee weapon, but sometimes he fires a rocket to damage multiple enemies in the same group. He can also blast a single opponent for massive damage.

Exit the temple and teleport to the Grand Shrine. Run to see the Great Shinto Priest and you see that everybody has been turned to stone. The priest is barely alive and gives you the Sacred Tear. After that, he turns to stone.

Before you hightail it out of there, talk to the Great Shinto Priest again. Of course since he's been turned to stone there's no response, but something catches your eye on the desk. Take the object and you acquire the Priest's Key. Use it on the treasure box to the right for another Dragon Doll.

Exit the temple area and follow the grassy path south. Follow this green path to a ramp into the mountains. Move along the mountain path as it winds north and west.

When the trail widens, you see a Dragon Doll on top of a rocky ledge on the left side. Use the Giant Hammer to grow large. In your giant form you can look at it and add the doll to your inventory.

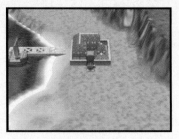

Teleport to Seapool and prepare for a rough journey. Rest up at the inn and save your progress at the church.

Board your vessel and sail west toward the island where you found the Giant Hammer in the sea. When you see the dock on the center island this time, park at it.

KING OF THE DEMONS LAIR

Walk north on the sandy beach and you come to a giant white cave. That cave takes you to the King of the Demons. There's no turning back now.

Encounters

Webman

Crab

The Webman won't hit you too hard in a melee battle, but his magic is deadly. Take out this creature before he gets a shot off. The Crab is not that difficult an opponent. Deal with it last if possible.

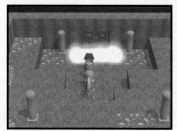

Enter the cave, a large cavern with gray pillars. Walk straight ahead and touch the glowing evil fire blocking the double doors. Look at it to use the Sacred Tear to make it disappear.

Encounters

Undead

Necromancer

Living Armor

Bone Dragon

Lizard Knight

Death Hound

Animated Blade

Frenzied Spider

The Necromancer is one mean creature. Its melee attack is nothing compared to its attack spells, which can kill a member of your party. One spell is very strong, but hits only one member. The other spell is extremely powerful and hits every member of the group.

Concentrate all your attacks and defeat the Necromancer before attacking the Undead and Living Armor it travels with. The Undead can be mean, too, but it just hits you with a sword. The Living Armor is probably the weakest creature

you'll fight in the cave. It doesn't hit particularly hard and it doesn't have that many health points.

The Bone Dragon is a mighty beast that can do a lot of damage. But if Cocona uses her Sunbeam Staff and Bulgil gets off an attack, the Bone Dragon is defeated before it gets a chance to harm you.

The Lizard Knight is tough. Not only can he take a vicious swipe at you, but he also can cast a spell to improve his defenses. He is a good candidate to target first.

Take the Death Hound to the pound. It sprays its hot breath on your group, taking away valuable health.

The Animated Blade and Frenzied Spider like to attack together. Luckily, they shouldn't be too difficult to defeat. Target the spider first, then move to the blades.

After the evil fire is gone, go through the double doors. Follow the corridor on the other side and pass the stairs leading down. They lead to an empty room.

At a fork in the road, you can go straight, up, or down. Go straight and at the end you're greeted with a Gemstone Ring in a treasure box.

Return to the crossroads and head north. It might not look like a path, but step into the black wall ahead to find another trail.

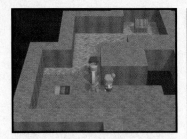

In the next room, follow the trail to the left, past the stairs and to the end. There you can open a treasure box for a Windy Shield.

Go down the stairs you just passed and follow the new trail to the right. Follow it to the north and open the treasure box for a Watery Shield.

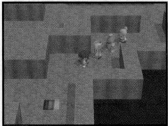

With the shield in your inventory, follow the tunnel south. Down there you discover another set of stairs.

The orange lava looks dangerous, but it can't hurt you. Follow the path west, then south. When you can't go any farther south, move to the west and climb the stairs.

In the next area, the trail leads you south, then west. When the trail splits, take the north fork and climb the stairs.

In the next room, climb the stairs and you get to a large cavern. To your north is a treasure box containing a Scorched Shield. Now fall into the dark crack next to the treasure box.

You fall into a separate area. Follow the passageway left and, when it splits, follow it down. A Swimsuit and King's Crown await you in the treasure boxes. Return to the split and take the northern trail.

This northern trail splits north and south. Go south first and open the box for 7,600 in gold. You hit the jackpot! Now go north, around the stairs, and through the dark entryway. A Withered Staff is in the treasure box there. Use it as an item in battle to heal a party member.

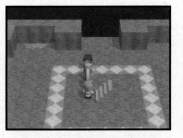

Climb the stairs you passed earlier, and head east. After the pillar-lined hall you find some stairs to descend. You end up in a large room with a square in the center. Forget about the square and head through the dark opening to the north.

EVIL'S PALACE

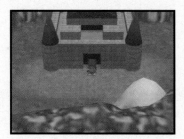

You made it through the cave and are at the front door of the King of the Demons. Don't be fooled by his nice-looking castle—it is pure evil inside. Walk through the front door when you're ready.

Hooligan received the Penguin Doll!

After you enter the castle, exit and teleport back to Seapool to save your progress and refill your health at the inn. Talk to the clown next to the inn and buy his doll for 30,000 gold. What a deal!

Please let me have it – I'll give you this ugly dragon doll in exchange! Please!

Teleport to Sankerest Castle and talk to the king's daughter in the throne room. Trade her your newly acquired doll for the Dragon Doll on the table.

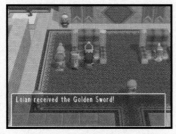

Loian received the Golden Sword!

Talk to the king about your journey. It is not good news, but he makes talking about it worth your while by giving you a Golden Sword. It will fetch a pretty penny at the shop. Talk to the queen and she gives you the Holy Dagger!

Teleport back to Evil's Palace. You are ready to face the worst bad guy of them all, the King of the Demons. Walk inside the castle.

Encounters

Grumpy Stature

Dark Messenger

Wrath

Beast

Cyclops

Reaver

Dragon

The Grumpy Stature is a mean-looking creature, but the sight of him means you're getting closer to the King of the Demons. He's not too tough, so just focus your attacks and the Grumpy Stature will be dust in no time.

The Dark Messenger brings nothing but bad news and a lot of pain. He strikes quickly, so focus all your attacks on him in the hope that he's dead by the next round. Sometimes he travels with his friend the Reaver. The Reaver is just as deadly, but is not as quick on the attack as the Dark Messenger.

The Wrath is a force to be reckoned with. It packs a mean attack and it strikes quickly. Focus all your group members on killing it, and you should live to retell the tale.

The Beast is a horrible creature. Its attack can harm your whole group. Kill the monster before it can sink its claws into you. Luckily, it doesn't have many health points.

The Cyclops might look friendly with his big smile, but he carries a big club. And when he brings it down on your head you feel a lot of pain...if you're still alive.

The Dragon likes to strike hard and fast, but it attacks alone. The combined efforts of your party can destroy it quickly.

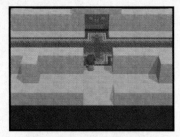

After you enter the castle, walk through the double doors ahead of you. In the next room, walk through another set of double doors.

The red carpet is rolled out for you. You don't walk in very far before the doors behind you slam shut. You can try walking to the end to get out, but a poisonous fog fills the air and knocks your party unconscious.

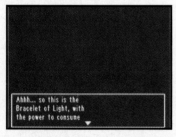

An evil voice is heard in the darkness. Whoever is speaking just stole your Bracelet of Light.

You awake in Sankerest Castle. How did you get there? Oh, well, you're safe for now. Try as you might, you can't get out. The front door is locked, by order of the king.

Go to the basement and check the treasure boxes. They're not the best items in the world, but you get a Lizard Tail, a Spider Web, a Bat Wing, a Gemstone Ring, a Cockroach Leg, and a Mantis Eye. Why would the king put such foul things in those treasure boxes?

Let's go talk to him. Make you way to the throne room and talk to the king. He says he's given up fighting the King of the Demons! What's going on here? Talk to anybody around and they seem to be smitten with the King of the Demons.

This is no place for you. Check the cupboards in the back right corner for 5,800 gold and a pair of Swift Boots. Look at the wall behind the throne and exit through the secret passage.

Check the treasure boxes along the way for an Unholy Necklace and a Magic Mushroom. Continue to follow the path to the secret exit outside.

What the...where are you? This isn't Sankerest Castle. You're back at Evil's Palace! Run south, then west to enter through the front door again.

Talk to the purple creature to start a fight. Yep, this isn't the castle. Defeat the creature and move through the double doors to find two more creatures. Talk to them before you put them down. Move through the next set of doors.

NOTE

You don't have to fight the purple creatures if you don't want to. Just ignore them and don't talk to them; they won't give you any trouble. But do you really want to let evil live?

Go down the set of stairs in front of you. Those two thieves are locked away. Run to the gate to open it and get some info from them. Before they leave, they say the King of the Demons is in a secret location.

Go back up the stairs and head to the left or right. The gray wall you find is really the back of a staircase. Walk your party south, then have them climb the stairs.

Move into the center room. In the back of the room, push the gray block to the side to open the treasure boxes for Stormy Armor and a Phoenix Feather.

With loot in hand, make your way south and climb some more stairs. In the next room, climb the large set of stairs against the left wall first. At the end, you can fall to the same platform as the treasure box with the Sun Skirt.

Fall from that platform and climb the small set of stairs this time. You end up in a large room with a scary picture on the wall. Walk to the back left or right corner, where you can see a black hole in the wall.

Next to the black hole is a large gray block. Push this block to the center of the painting. Climb the small wall in the center of the room and step on the block. Step toward the painting, and your party walks into it.

NOTE

You can't use your Escape or Teleport spell once you have entered the painting. You'll have to exit the painting first if you want to cast those spells.

You have found the King of the Demon's secret hiding area! Enter the palace doors to arrive in a long room. Move through the small doorway on your left. Follow the side hallway to a treasure box with a Dragon Doll inside.

Encounters

Centaur

Evoker

The Centaur gallops at you with its lance pointed at your belly. It charges so fast you just have to take the attack. Even after your party attacks it, the Centaur might have enough life left in it for another attack. If anyone is seriously injured, have that member defend while the others press the attack.

Encounters Continued

The Evoker might look like it is there to amuse you, but it really only has dirty deeds on its agenda. Pummel it with swords and damaging spells before it causes you a lot of damage.

Return to the main room and head north. In the next room is a platform with a golden circle. Before you step on it, head to the room on the right for the Burning Blade in a treasure box. That sword is perfect for your hero!

Before you go on to meet the King of the Demons, attend to one last item. Now that you have all seven Dragon Dolls, so go to the Dragon Temple. Backtrack to the point where you entered the giant picture. Then you can use Escape to get outside and teleport to Hezan.

Follow the high mountain trail to the south of Hezan. When you leave the trail you get to a dock where your boat awaits. Jump in and sail south. Soon you arrive at a small island.

Dock your boat and enter the temple. This place is just like the Wooden Doll and Robot Temples. Look at each platform and place the Dragon Doll down.

After you place the seventh Dragon Doll, a Dragon comes to life on the center platform. The Dragon's name is Draig and he wants to join your group. Kick Bulgil to the curb, and you have a new group member.

Teleport to Seapool so you can rest up and save your progress. When you're ready, Teleport to Evil's Palace and make your way through the castle until you get to the area with the golden circle again.

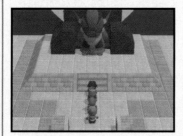

Step on the golden circle and you are transported to Jadece's throne room. Climb the tall set of steps to find the King of the Demons at the top. That guy is huge!

TIP

Before you start the fight, take any items you need from the bag and put them on a character. You won't have access to any items in the bag after the fight begins.

Three items are important to have on hand. Give your hero the Fruit of Ages. Give everyone in your party Magic Mushrooms to replenish magic, and give them Phoenix Feathers to bring the dead back to life. You need most of these items as you fight the final two bosses.

Caution

Do not fight Jadece unless someone in your party has the Group Heal spell. Loian gains it at Level 20. When cast, it heals everyone in your party. Without it, your group members die horrible deaths, one by one.

If you don't have the spell yet, just keep fighting the monsters you fought before to get more experience, and eventually the Group Heal.

Talk to Jadece to begin the battle. This won't be easy or quick. He is the King of the Demons, after all. Jadece can cast spells to hit one member of your party or all four at once. These spells are so powerful that if one of your party members is injured, they wind up dead after one of his spell attacks.

You can win; just follow a simple pattern. Attack with your hero's weapon to cause whatever damage he can. Cocona should shoot a ball of flame from her staff. And your Dragon friend is always good for a powerful attack.

Loian isn't that powerful with his weapon or his offensive spells. He does have a great spell in the Group Heal, though. Have him cast it after the battle begins.

No matter what punches Jadece throws, you always start the next round with your group at full health and ready to go. Before Loian runs out of magic points, use a Magic Mushroom on him to refill them. Continue fighting, using the same technique.

After what seems like forever, Jadece starts having problems and everyone exits the encounter. That's good news and bad news. The bad news is that Liavo, Jadece's flunky, shows up. The good news is that he wants you to kick some Jadece butt. Liavo uses the Bracelet of Light to rob Jadece of his powers.

Without his magical powers, Jadece isn't nearly as strong. He can still hit with his claws and do some damage to one group member per round. Save your magic power for now and have everyone attack. If someone takes a little too much damage, use an individual healing spell on them.

After a few rounds of battle, you finally defeat Jadece. That sure was nice of Liavo, and he expresses his appreciation.

Unfortunately, now he wants control. And control for him means your death. He grows to an enormous size and the last battle begins.

This fight is similar to the previous one. Use your hero's Tsunami spell to inflict the most damage on Liavo. Draig uses whatever attack he feels necessary, because you can't control him. Have Loian continue to use Group Heal to heal everyone in the group. Most important, have Cocona use her spells to increase Draig's attack power and also to increase the group's defenses.

The biggest problem is that Liavo can cast Berserk on himself. When he's Berserk, he can kill most of your party members with one hit. Keep Loian healing, and have your hero and Cocona defend. If they get hit while defending and they have full health, they probably won't die. Use a Phoenix Feather on any fallen comrade. When the Berserk ends, resume your previous method of attack.

TIP

When everyone starts to get low on magic, use your hero's Fruit of Ages to replenish the group's health and magic. During this turn, Loian does not need to cast Group Heal.

Finally, Liavo dies. It was a rough fight but you managed to get through it. Looks like they underestimated the powers of humans. You truly are the hero!

Seramus and your ancestor show up to congratulate your victory. Without the powers of the King of the Demons, the castle will soon be nothing more than rubble. The two of them transport you to safety as the castle disappears.

After a visit to the Grand Shrine, you visit Sankerest Castle. Go upstairs to the throne room to find the king, your parents, and a lot of well-wishers.

He is pleased with what you've done. And what better way to celebrate than with a feast! After you chat with everyone, talk with the king to get the next dish.

You're offered a place to stay at the castle. It's a generous offer from the king, but you belong in San Moreek at the inn. At least until the next adventure.

MAPS

You have many different maps to choose from when creating your own RPG. Use any of the maps as is or modify them to suit your needs. Experiment with the options and have fun. To enter the Map database, select "Graphics," then "Map Editor" from the main menu.

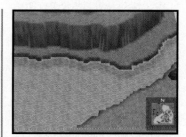

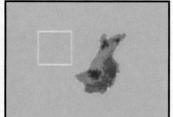
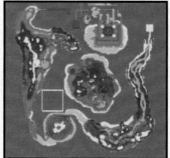
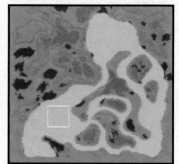

**Map #0: Preset World
(Beginning Island)**

**Map #2: Continent 1
(Standard)**

Map #4: Ruins (Island)

**Map #6: Barren Cliffs
(Craved Lake)**

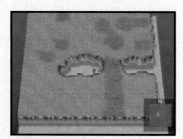
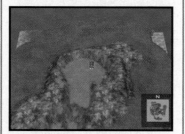

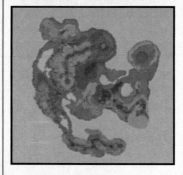
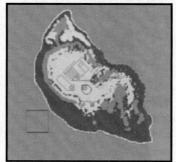
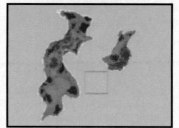
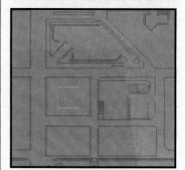

**Map #1: Preset Town
(Beginning Town)**

**Map #3: Continent 2
(Volcanic)**

**Map #5: Isle (Two Tropical
Islands)**

Map #7: Urban (Modern)

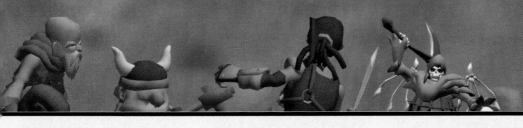
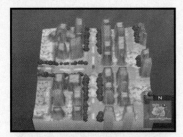

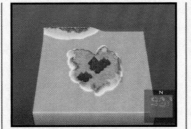

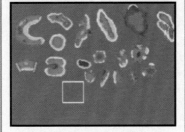

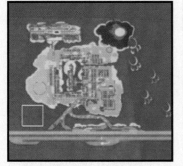

**Map #8: Battlegrounds
(Futuristic Monster)**

Map #9: Islands (18 Assorted)

Map #10: Assorted (13 Mixed)

**Map #11: Fun (Interesting
Creations)**

DUNGEONS

You have many models of dungeons to choose from, ranging from an ordinary room to a spooky watchtower. Find a dungeon model that suits your needs, and optionally modify your selection to better fit the story of your RPG. To enter the Dungeon database, select "Graphics" then "Dungeon Editor" from the main menu.

Dungeon #0: Preset Shops (Preset Shops)

Dungeon #1: Inn Floor 1 & 2 (Preset Inn)

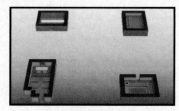

Dungeon #2: Castle 1 (Outside Castle Gate)

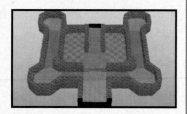

Dungeon #3: Castle 2 (First Floor)

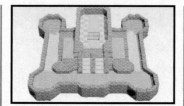

Dungeon #4: Castle 3 (Second Floor)

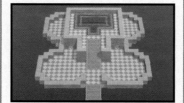

Dungeon #5: Castle 4 (Throne Room)

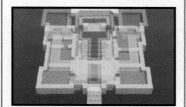

Dungeon #6: Castle 5 (Royal Chambers)

Dungeon #7: Tower 1 (First to Third Floor)

Dungeon #8: Tower 2 (Fourth to Sixth Floor)

Dungeon #9: Tower 3 (Winding Stairs)

Dungeon #10: Tower 4 (Mystical 3F Staircase)

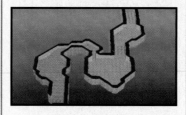

Dungeon #11: Cavern 1 (Rock Cavern Passageway)

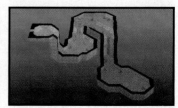

Dungeon #12: Cavern 2 (Rock Cavern Dead End)

Dungeon #13: Ruins 1 (Halls)

Dungeon #14: Ruins 2 (Treasury)

Dungeon #15: Dungeon (Four Rooms)

Dungeon #16: Underground (Passageway Two Rooms)

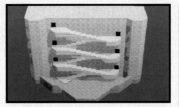

Dungeon #19: Pillaged House (Destroyed)

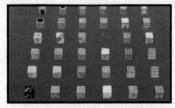

Dungeon #22: Fire Escape (Six Floors)

Dungeon #25: Mixed Blocks (Textured Six Blocks)

Dungeon #17: Market (Five Counters)

Dungeon #20: Maze (32x29 Blocks)

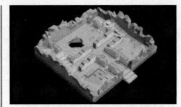

Dungeon #23: Mixed Blocks (Textured Single Blocks)

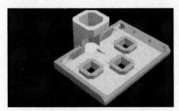

Dungeon #18: Water Storage (Four Wells)

Dungeon #21: Academy (Training Grounds)

Dungeon #24: Mixed Blocks (Textured Four Blocks)

BUILDINGS

Buildings are the main structures in your cities or villages. Choose from a wide range of buildings—big to small, ordinary to weird. The buildings you add to your RPG affect gameplay, so choose wisely. To enter the Building database, select "Graphics," then "Building Editor" from the main menu.

Building #0: House

Building #1: Red Roof Cottage

Building #2: Red Roof Building

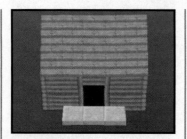

Building #3: Log Cabin

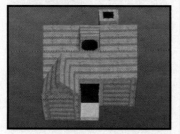

Building #4: Log Lodge

Building #5: Shelter 1

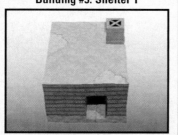

Building #6: Shelter 2

Building #7: Shelter 3

Building #8: Large House

Building #9: Abandoned Building

Building #10: Winter Cabin

Building #11: Hut

Building #12: Gazebo

Building #13: Raised Hut

Building #14: Jail

Building #15: Fortress

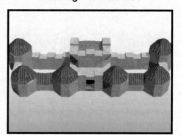

Building #16: Castle

Building #17: Cathedral

Building #18: Monastery

Building #23: Barracks

Building #28: Shop 3 (Interior)

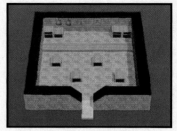
Building #33: Tavern (Interior)

Building #19: Beach House

Building #24: Prison

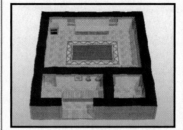
Building #29: Shop 4 (Interior)

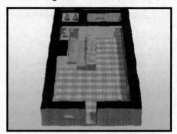
Building #34: Restaurant (Interior)

Building #20: Town Hall

Building #25: Warehouse

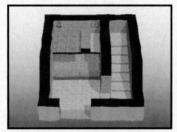
Building #30: Shop 5 (Interior)

Building #35: Cathedral (Interior)

Building #21: Tower

Building #26: Shop 1 (Interior)

Building #31: Mansion 1 (Interior)

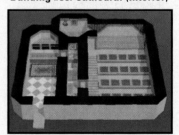
Building #36: Theater (Interior)

Building #22: Farmhouse (Barn)

Building #27: Shop 2 (Interior)

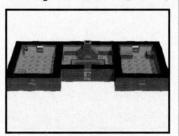
Building #32: Mansion 2 (Interior)

Building #37: School (Interior)

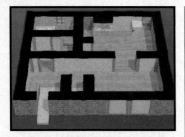

Building #38: House (Interior)

Building #43: Bell Tower

Building #48: Giant Vase

Building #53: Cannon

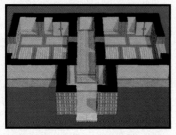

Building #39: Dojo (Interior)

Building #44: Monument

Building #49: Gate 1

Building #54: Airship 1

Building #40: Tea Room (Interior)

Building #45: Observation Tower

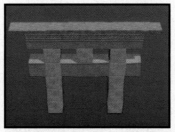

Building #50: Gate 2

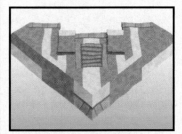

Building #55: Airship 2

Building #41: Stone Bridge (Small)

Building #46: Stone Monument 1

Building #51: Subway Entrance

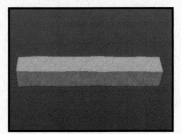

Building #56: Pier

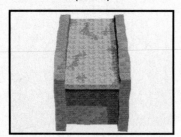

Building #42: Stone Bridge (Large)

Building #47: Stone Monument 2

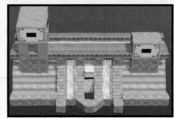

Building #52: Dam

Building/Dungeon Textures

When you build a dungeon or building, you want it to look a certain way. If it's an old building, you want it to have the look of broken stone. If it's a barn, you want wood. You have hundreds of building textures to choose from to give your building the specific look you want. To enter the Texture database, select "Graphics/Dungeon Editor or Building Editor" from the main menu.

Whether you want to modify an existing model or create something from scratch, choose the edit option. Once your grid is formed, press R2 to bring up the textures. For alternate textures, press L2 while holding R2.

LOWER TEXTURES

Texture #	Name	Texture	Texture #	Name	Texture	Texture #	Name	Texture	Texture #	Name	Texture
0	Black		16	Wood P		32	Wall Frame D		48	Wood Aged G	
1	Wood A		17	Wood Q		33	Wall Frame E		49	Wood Aged H	
2	Wood B		18	Wood R		34	Wall Frame F		50	Wood Aged I	
3	Wood C		19	Log A		35	Wall Frame G		51	Wood Aged J	
4	Wood D		20	Log B		36	Wall Frame H		52	Wall Aged A	
5	Wood E		21	Log C		37	Wall Frame I		53	Wall Aged B	
6	Wood F		22	Log D		38	Wall Frame J		54	Wall Aged C	
7	Wood G		23	Wood Design A		39	Wall Frame K		55	Wall Aged D	
8	Wood H		24	Wood Design B		40	Wall Frame L		56	Wall Aged E	
9	Wood I		25	Wood Design C		41	Wall Frame M		57	Wall Aged F	
10	Wood J		26	Wood Design D		42	Wood Aged A		58	Wall Aged G	
11	Wood K		27	Wood Design E		43	Wood Aged B		59	Wall Aged H	
12	Wood L		28	Wall		44	Wood Aged C		60	Wooden Door	
13	Wood M		29	Wall Frame A		45	Wood Aged D		61	Roof Tile A	
14	Wood N		30	Wall Frame B		46	Wood Aged E		62	Roof Tile B	
15	Wood O		31	Wall Frame C		47	Wood Aged F		63	Roof Log A	

Texture #	Name	Texture	Texture #	Name	Texture	Texture #	Name	Texture	Texture #	Name	Texture
64	Roof Log B		85	Heavy Log E		106	Stone Design D		127	Stone Wall H	
65	Roof Bamboo A		86	Heavy Log F		107	Sand A		128	Stone Wall I	
66	Roof Bamboo B		87	Number 0		108	Sand B		129	Stone Wall J	
67	Roof Bamboo C		88	Number 1		109	Sand C		130	Stone Wall K	
68	Roof Thatch A		89	Number 2		110	Sand D		131	Stone	
69	Roof Thatch B		90	Number 3		111	Sand E		132	Stone Symbol A	
70	Roof Wood		91	Number 4		112	Sand F		133	Stone Symbol B	
71	Roof Stone		92	Number 5		113	Sand G		134	Stone Symbol C	
72	Roof Dark		93	Number 6		114	Brick		135	Stone Symbol D	
73	Roof Bright A		94	Number 7		115	Brick Entrance		136	Stone Symbol E	
74	Roof Bright B		95	Number 8		116	Brick Cracked		137	Stone Symbol F	
75	Floor Wood A		96	Number 9		117	Brick Aged		138	Stone Symbol G	
76	Floor Wood B		97	Stone A		118	Cracked Stone A		139	Stone Symbol H	
77	Floor Wood C		98	Stone B		119	Cracked Stone B		140	Hieroglyph	
78	Floor Wood D		99	Stone C		120	Stone Wall A		141	Gray Wall	
79	Floor Wood E		100	Stone D		121	Stone Wall B		142	Tile A	
80	Floor Wood F		101	Stone E		122	Stone Wall C		143	Tile B	
81	Heavy Log A		102	Stone F		123	Stone Wall D		144	Tile C	
82	Heavy Log B		103	Stone Design A		124	Stone Wall E		145	Tile D	
83	Heavy Log C		104	Stone Design B		125	Stone Wall F		146	Tile E	
84	Heavy Log D		105	Stone Design C		126	Stone Wall G		147	Tile F	

Texture #	Name	Texture	Texture #	Name	Texture	Texture #	Name	Texture	Texture #	Texture
148	Stair Left		169	Door H		190	Ice B		9	
149	Stair Center		170	Door I		191	Ice C		10	
150	Stair Right		171	Door J		192	Ice D		11	
151	Moss A		172	Door K		193	Ice E		12	
152	Moss B		173	Door L		194	Ice F		13	
153	Log Aged		174	Door M		195	Gold		14	
154	Stone Aged		175	Door N		196	Lava		15	
155	Bench A		176	Door O		197	Cushion		16	
156	Bench B		177	Mat A		198	Stained Glass		17	
157	Turtle Shell		178	Mat B		199	Transparent		18	
158	Ivy		179	Mat C					19	
159	Metallic Sand		180	Mat D					20	
160	Wall Clay A		181	Mat E					21	
161	Wall Clay B		182	Mat F					22	
162	Door A		183	Mat Aged A					23	
163	Door B		184	Mat Aged B					24	
164	Door C		185	Mat Aged C					25	
165	Door D		186	Mat Aged D					26	
166	Door E		187	Mat Aged E					27	
167	Door F		188	Mat Aged F					28	
168	Door G		189	Ice A					29	

UPPER TEXTURES

Texture #	Texture
0	
1	
2	
3	
4	
5	
6	
7	
8	

Texture #	Texture	Texture #	Texture	Texture #	Texture	Texture #	Texture	Texture #	Texture	Texture #	Texture
30		51		72		93		114			
31		52		73		94		115			
32		53		74		95		116			
33		54		75		96		117			
34		55		76		97		118			
35		56		77		98		119			
36		57		78		99		120			
37		58		79		100		121			
38		59		80		101		122			
39		60		81		102		123			
40		61		82		103		124			
41		62		83		104		125			
42		63		84		105		126			
43		64		85		106		127			
44		65		86		107		128			
45		66		87		108		129			
46		67		88		109		130			
47		68		89		110		131			
48		69		90		111		132			
49		70		91		112		133			
50		71		92		113		134			

Texture #	Texture	Texture #	Texture	Texture #	Texture	Texture #	Texture	Texture #	Texture	Texture #	Texture
135		148		161		174		187			
136		149		162		175		188			
137		150		163		176		189			
138		151		164		177		190			
139		152		165		178		191			
140		153		166		179		192			
141		154		167		180		193			
142		155		168		181		194			
143		156		169		182		195			
144		157		170		183		196			
145		158		171		184					
146		159		172		185					
147		160		173		186					

MAP TEXTURES

When you build a map you want certain areas to have a certain look. Snow should look like snow, dirt like dirt. You can use these textures on your map to make the story environment look more believable. The textures you choose can establish the feel of your map.

To enter the Terrain Texture database, select "Graphics/Map Editor/Custom/Texture/Type." This takes you to the full list of landscape textures.

After "Custom," select "Trees/Texture" or "Sea/Texture" instead of "Texture" to access the specific textures for those areas.

LANDSCAPE TEXTURES

Texture #	Name	Texture
0	Rock A	
1	Rock B	
2	Rock C	
3	Rock D	
4	Rock E	
5	Rock F	
6	Rock Snowy A	
7	Rock Snowy B	
8	Rock Snowy C	
9	Rock Snowy D	
10	Rock Snowy E	
11	Rock Snowy F	
12	Rock Snowy G	
13	Sand A	
14	Sand B	
15	Granite	

Texture #	Name	Texture
16	Grass Rough	
17	Dirt Rough	
18	Grass Light	
19	Grass Dark	
20	Dirt A	
21	Dirt B	
22	Dirt C	
23	River Dry A	
24	River Dry B	
25	River Dry C	
26	Volcanic A	
27	Volcanic B	
28	Volcanic C	
29	Volcanic D	
30	Pitted A	
31	Pitted B	

Texture #	Name	Texture
32	Pitted C	
33	Speckled A	
34	Speckled B	
35	Speckled C	
36	Speckled D	
37	Speckled E	
38	Snow A	
39	Snow B	
40	Soil A	
41	Soil B	
42	Soil C	
43	Scale A	
44	Scale B	
45	Scale C	
46	Scale D	
47	Scale E	

Texture #	Name	Texture
48	Scale F	
49	Fiber A	
50	Fiber B	
51	Fiber C	
52	Clay A	
53	Clay B	
54	Clay C	
55	Striped A	
56	Striped B	
57	Striped C	
58	Striped D	
59	Striped E	
60	Striped F	
61	Paved A	
62	Paved B	
63	Paved C	

Texture #	Name	Texture
64	Paved D	
65	Paved E	
66	Brick A	
67	Brick B	
68	Brick C	
69	Brick D	
70	Brick E	
71	Brick F	
72	Floorboard A	
73	Floorboard B	
74	Floorboard C	
75	Floorboard D	
76	Floorboard E	
77	Weathered A	
78	Weathered B	
79	Weathered C	
80	Weathered D	
81	Woven A	
82	Woven B	
83	Woven C	
84	Woven D	

Texture #	Name	Texture
85	Tile A	
86	Tile B	
87	Tile C	
88	Tile D	
89	Moss A	
90	Moss B	
91	Moss C	
92	Moss D	
93	Moss E	
94	Stone Paved A	
95	Stone Paved B	
96	Stone Paved C	
97	Stone Paved D	
98	Rainbow	
99	No Design	

TREE TEXTURES

Texture #	Name	Texture
1	Deep Green	
2	Dry Green	
3	Autumn A	
4	Autumn B	
5	Snow A	
6	Snow B	
7	Fruit	
8	Aged Leaves	
9	Rainbow	
10	No Design	

SEA TEXTURES

Texture #	Name	Texture
1	Sea A	
2	Sea B	
3	Sea C	
4	Sea D	
5	Lava A	
6	Lava B	
7	River A	
8	River B	
9	Rainbow	
10	No Design	

OBJECTS

Objects fill your RPG with life; that's why there are so many from which to choose. They might not seem as important as the map you make or the buildings you put down, but the objects you scatter about give your RPG a unique feel. The story you create becomes more interesting as your characters interact with objects. To enter the Object database select "Graphics," then "Object Models" from the main menu.

Some object models have animated textures or built in actions associated with them. The objects marked with "AC" have actions, while the objects marked with "AN" have animated textures.

Object #0: Barrel

Object #4: Vase A

Object #8: Coin Silver (AC)

Object #12: Pile of Gold

Object #1: Crate

Object #5: Vase B

Object #9: Coin Gold (AC)

Object #13: Grass

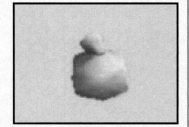

Object #2: Bag

Object #6: Chest (AC)

Object #10: Coin Bronze (AC)

Object #14: Weeds

Object #3: Sack

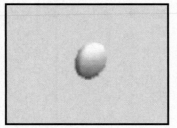

Object #7: Coin Small (AC)

Object #11: Magic Lamp

Object #15: Flower

Object #16: Vegetable

Object #17: Mushroom

Object #18: Flower Bed

Object #19: Flower Planter

Object #20: Potted Plant

Object #21: Potted Tree

Object #22: Tall Weed

Object #23: Sunflower

Object #24: Cactus

Object #25: Tree Small

Object #26: Tree Large

Object #27: Tree Stump Half

Object #28: Tree Dead

Object #29: Tree Palm

Object #30: Stairs A Up

Object #31: Stairs A Down

Object #32: Stairs B Center

Object #33: Stairs B Right

Object #34: Stairs B Left

Object #38: Pier End

Object #42: Log Bridge

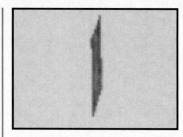

Object #47: Waterfall Side B (AN)

Object #35: Stairs B Down

Object #39: Pier Center

Object #43: River (AN)

Object #48: Wooden Sign

Object #36: Stairs C

Object #40: Rope Bridge End

Object #44: Waterfall Upper (AN)

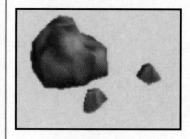

Object #49: Rocks

Object #37: Bridge

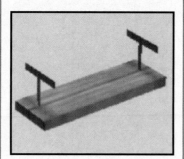

Object #41: Rope Bridge Mid

Object #45: Waterfall Mid (AN)

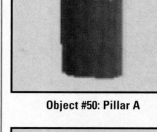

Object #50: Pillar A

Object #46: Waterfall Side A (AN)

Object #51: Pillar B

Object #52: Fence A

Object #57: Bonfire

Object #62: Propeller A (AC)

Object #67: Tracks Straight

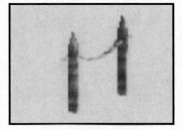

Object #53: Fence B

Object #58: Crack Extension

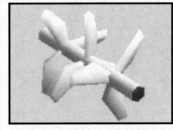

Object #63: Propeller B (AC)

Object #68: Tracks Curved

Object #54: Fence C

Object #59: Crack (AC)

Object #64: Propeller C (AC)

Object #69: Tracks Broken

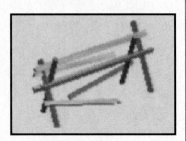

Object #55: Fence D

Object #60: Gear A (AC)

Object #65: Drill A (AC)

Object #70: Tracks End

Object #56: Lumber

Object #61: Gear B (AC)

Object #66: Drill B (AC)

Object #71: Flag

Object #72: Weather Vein (AC)

Object #73: Switch (AC)

Object #74: Rock Pillar

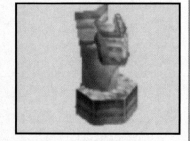

Object #75: Talisman Statue

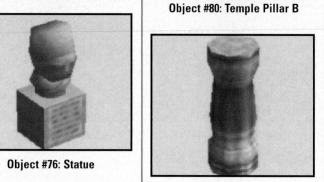

Object #76: Statue

Object #77: Lantern Pedestal

Object #78: Rock Monument

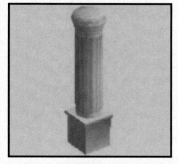

Object #79: Temple Pillar A

Object #80: Temple Pillar B

Object #81: Interior Pillar

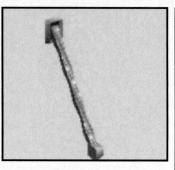

Object #82: Bridge Chain L

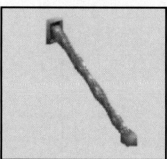

Object #83: Bridge Chain R

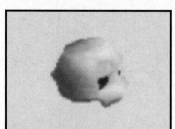

Object #84: Skull

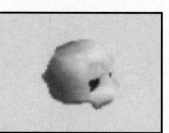

Object #85: Coffin

Object #86: Tombstone A

Object #87: Tombstone B

Object #88: Tombstone C

Object #89: Broken Wall

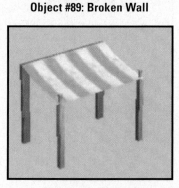

Object #90: Canopy

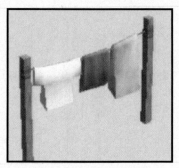

Object #91: Clothesline

Object #92: Water Trough

Object #97: Crater

Object #102: Gate A

Object #107: Crystal Form

Object #93: Well

Object #98: Cannon

Object #103: Gate B

Object #108: Rock Face

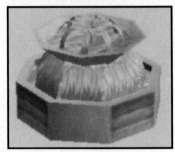

Object #94: Fountain (AC)

Object #99: Stained Glass

Object #104: Tent

Object #109: Sign Weapon

Object #95: Watermill (AC)

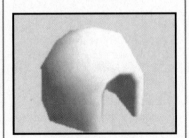

Object #100: Large Clock

Object #105: Igloo

Object #110: Sign Armor

Object #96: Windmill (AC)

Object #101: Bell Tower

Object #106: Snowman

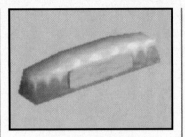

Object #111: Sign Item

Object #112: Sign Inn

Object #117: Hoe

Object #122: Axe

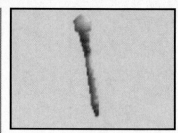

Object #127: Scepter A

Object #113: Sign Tavern

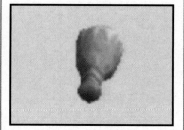

Object #118: Club

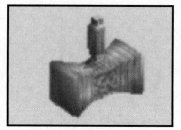

Object #123: Hammer

Object #128: Scepter B

Object #114: Sign Magic

Object #119: Sword

Object #124: Spear Rack

Object #129: Royal Flag

Object #115: Sign Generic

Object #120: Broken Sword

Object #125: Whip Wall

Object #130: Helmet

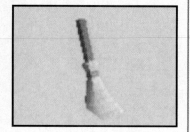

Object #116: Broom

Object #121: Swords Wall

Object #126: Bow and Arrows

Object #131: Armor

Object #132: Gauntlets

Object #137: Window A

Object #142: Window F

Object #147: Window Inside D

Object #133: Shield

Object #138: Window B

Object #143: Window G

Object #148: Window Inside E

Object #134: Chimney A

Object #139: Window C

Object #144: Window Inside A

Object #149: Window Inside F

Object #135: Chimney B

Object #140: Window D

Object #145: Window Inside B

Object #150: Window Inside G

Object #136: Chimney C

Object #141: Window E (AC)

Object #146: Window Inside C

Object #151: Door Single A (AC)

RPG MAKER II PRIMA'S OFFICIAL STRATEGY GUIDE

Object #152: Door Single B (AC)

Object #153: Door Single C (AC)

Object #154: Door Double A (AC)

Object #155: Door Double B (AC)

Object #156: Doorway A

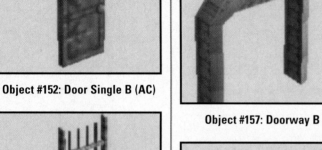

Object #157: Doorway B

Object #158: Rug A

Object #159: Rug B

Object #160: Rug C

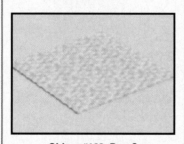

Object #161: Curtain

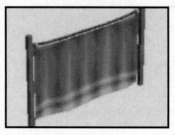

Object #162: Notice

Object #163: Map

Object #164: Picture

Object #165: Tapestry

Object #166: Shelf Wall

Object #167: Candles Wall

Object #168: Torch Wall

Object #169: Note

Object #170: Book Closed

Object #171: Book Open

Object #172: Scroll

Object #177: Stool

Object #182: Tree Stump

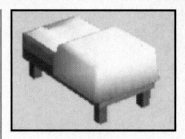

Object #187: Bed A

Object #173: Crystal Ball

Object #178: Bench

Object #183: Table A

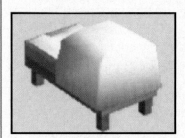

Object #188: Bed A Used

Object #174: Lamp

Object #179: Chair A

Object #184: Table B

Object #189: Bed B

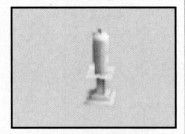

Object #175: Candle

Object #180: Chair B

Object #185: Table C

Object #190: Bed B Used

Object #176: Candle Floor

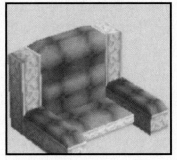

Object #181: Throne

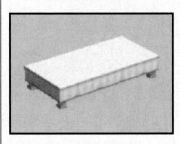

Object #186: Table D

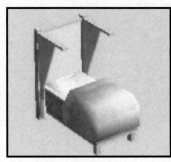

Object #191: Bed C

Object #192: Bed C Used

Object #193: Ladder

Object #194: Platform

Object #195: Mirror

Object #196: Stage

Object #197: Counter

Object #198: Counter Corner

Object #199: Dresser (AC)

Object #200: Armoire (AC)

Object #201: Dressing Table

Object #202: Grandfather Clock

Object #203: Cross

Object #204: Gazebo

Object #205: Fireplace

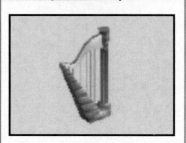

Object #206: Harp

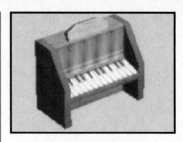

Object #207: Piano

Object #208: Bookshelf

Object #209: Bottle Cabinet

Object #210: Kitchen

Object #211: Plate

Object #212: Table Setting

Object #217: Pan and Cleaver

Object #222: Carriage Used

Object #227: Turtle (AC)

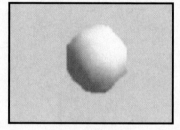

Object #213: Ball

Object #218: Pot

Object #223: Car

Object #228: Shark (AC)

Object #214: Bread Basket

Object #219: Sleigh

Object #224: Truck

Object #229: Whale (AC)

Object #215: Bottle

Object #220: Mine Cart

Object #225: Oyster

Object #230: Dragon Young (AC)

Object #216: Mug

Object #221: Carriage

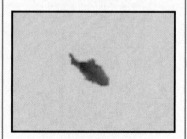

Object #226: Fish (AC)

Object #231: Floating Ice (AC)

Object #232: Driftwood (AC)

Object #233: Raft (AC)

Object #234: Boat Small (AC)

Object #235: Boat Large (AC)

Object #236: Boat Crashed (AC)

Object #237: Submarine (AC)

Object #238: Magic Carpet (AC)

Object #239: Cloud (AC)

Object #240: Airship (AC)

Object #241: Hot Air Balloon (AC)

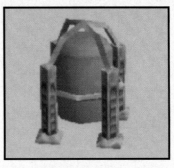

Object #242: Time Capsule (AC)

Object #243: Event Box

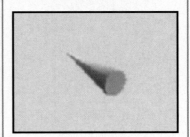

Object #244: Marker

Object #245: Village A

Object #246: Village B

Object #247: Village C

Object #248: Village D

Object #249: City A

Object #250: City B

Object #251: City C

Object #252: Castle A

Object #256: Tower B

Object #260: Tent

Object #263: Cave A

Object #253: Castle B

Object #257: Ruins

Object #261: Pyramid

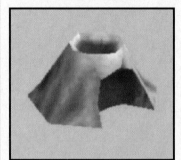

Object #264: Cave B

Object #254: Castle C

Object #258: Temple

Object #262: Igloos

Object #255: Tower A

Object #259: Fort

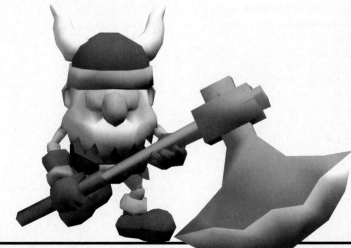

CHARACTERS

You can choose from many characters in *RPG Maker 2*—male or female, characters with different professions, even characters that are animals or objects. As you create your own RPG, take advantage of the diverse selection to make your story more exciting and more enjoyable. To enter the Character database, select "Graphics," then "Character Models" from the main menu. You can access and use the action that is described by selecting the Action field in the Character Editor, then by selecting "Special."

Character #0: Hero
Punch

Character #1:
Soldier Male

Two Handed Refusal
Character #2: Soldier Female

Spreads Both Arms
Character #3: Monk Male
Raises Hands Upward

Character #4:
Monk Female
Flicks Hair Back

Character #5:
Fighter Male
Jump Kick

Character #6: Fighter Female
Jump And Twist

Character #7: Sorcerer
Two Hand Casting Motion

Character #8: Sorceress
One Hand Casting Motion

Character #9: Priest
Two Hand Casting Motion

Character #10: Priestess
One Hand Casting Motion

Character #11: Hunter
Head Shake And One Hand Point

Character #12: Huntress
Head Shake And Two Hand Point

Character #13:
Merchant Male
Nod And One Hand Point

Character #14:
Merchant Female
Bow

Character #15:
Jester Male
Bow, Arms Spread

**Character #16:
Jester Female
Raises Each Hand Successively**

**Character #17: Pirate Captain
Nods To Either Side**

**Character #18: Pirate
Wind Up And Punch**

**Character #19: Sailor
Clicks Hand And Foot In Salute**

**Character #20: Cowboy
Two Handed Draw
And Fire**

**Character #21: Cowgirl
Two Handed Draw
And Fire**

**Character #22: Dancer
Raises Arm And Twirls**

**Character #23:
Nomad Male
Hop And Jump**

**Character #24:
Nomad Female
Long Stride**

**Character #25:
Nomad Leader
Nods With Hands
Behind Back**

**Character #26: King
Twist And Point**

**Character #27: Queen
Lowers Head, Hands
To Chest**

**Character #28: Prince
One Handed Dismissal**

**Character #29: Princess
Curtsey**

**Character #30: Knight
Clicks Hands And
Feet In Salute**

**Character #31: Robot A
Lifting Motion**

**Character #32: Robot B
Removes Armor, Forms
A Shield**

**Character #33: Baby
Rolls On Its Side**

Character #34: Child Male
Twists, Hands Outstretched

Character #38: Adult Male
Rubs Hands Together

Character #43: Waitress
Placing Motion

Character #48: Thin Male
Bends And Points

Character #35:
Child Female
Wobbles Hands Flailing

Character #39:
Adult Female
Leans Back, Hands Behind Back

Character #44: Clerk
Giving Motion

Character #49:
Eskimo Male
Nods, Hands Behind Back

Character #36:
Young Male
Nods, Points To The Side

Character #40: Old Male
Leans Forward On Cane

Character #45: Minister
Blesses Points Upward

Character #50:
Eskimo Female
Hop, Hands Outstretched

Character #37:
Young Female
Long Stride

Character #41: Old Female
Scolding Nod

Character #46: Barbarian
Lifting And Head Shake

Character #51:
Arabian Male
Arms Stretch, Head Slides

Character #42: Chef
Preparing/Cutting Motion

Character #47: Fat Male
Beats Belly

Character #52:
Arabian Female
Hands To Chest,
Head Slides

Character #53:
African Male
High Hop

Character #54: African Female
One Handed Slap

Character #55: Magistrate
One Hand Back Slap

Character #56: General
One Hand Slash

Character #57: Duchess
Nod

Character #58: Samurai
One Handed Dismissal

Character #59: Ninja Male
Back Flip

Character #60:
Ninja Female
Front Flip

Character #61: Imp
One Handed Punch

Character #62:
Student Male
Side To Side Glance

Character #63:
Student Female
Arches Back

Character #64: Male
Glances To Side,
Head Tilt

Character #65: Female
Points Each Hand
And Foot

Character #66:
Teacher Male
Points Behind And
Then Forward

Character #67:
Teacher Female
Points Upward And
Then Forward

Character #68: Professor
Shrugs

Character #69: Thief
Wobbles, Raises Arms Up

Character #74: Fairy
Arms To Shoulder, Than Outward

Character #79: Pharaoh
Hand And Head To
The Sky

Character #84: Guardian
Raises Hands Slightly

Character #70: God
Hop, Raises Arm

Character #75: Death
Scythe Rotates
Around Death

Character #80: Count
Looks Up And Hops

Character #85: Mermaid
Swimming Motion

Character #71: Goddess
Levitates

Character #76: Spirit
Head Rises Slowly

Character #81: Mummy
Falls Face To The Ground

Character #86: Wolf Man
Howls At The Moon

Character #72: Angel
Hops, Spins Around

Character #77: Fiend
Side To Side Glance

Character #82: Skeleton
Body Stretches Upward

Character #87: Bird Boy
Flaps Wings

Character #73: Demon
Hops, Spreads Arms

Character #78: Crusader
Raises Arms In Victory

Character #83: Treant
Marches

Character #88: Dog
Barks

Character #89: Cat
Cat Nap

Character #90: Pig
Skipping

Character #91: Sheep
Waddling

Character #92: Horse
Nodding Head

Character #93: Camel
Lowering Head

Character #94: Bird
Back Flip

Character #95: Chicken
Pecking At The Ground

Character #96: Penguin
Flaps Wings

Character #97: Ostrich
Waddles On Each Foot

Character #98:
Dragon Young
Exhale

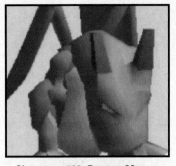

Character #99: Dragon Mature
Hop, Wings Flapping

Character #100: Squid
Hop With Flippers Flailing

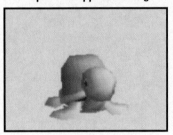

Character #101: Turtle
Crawl

Character #102: Sea Turtle
Swims

Character #103: Slime
Hops, Body Stretches

Character #104: Vase
Rocks

Character #105: Coffin Shakes

Character #106: Boss A Floats

Character #107: Boss B Floats

Character #108: Elf Male Head Sways

Character #109: Elf Female Head Sways

Character #110: Superhero Points

Character #111: Artist Flexes

Character #112: Magician Adjusts Glasses

Character #113: Cleric Taps Shield

Character #114: Pixie Front Flip

Character #115: Oracle Waves Staff

Enemies

What would an RPG be without a lot of scary monsters and creatures roaming about terrorizing the villagers? *RPG Maker 2* has plenty of enemies from which to choose. Some terrorize the countryside; some like to stick with the seas. Mix up your monsters to create exciting encounters for your heroes! To enter the Enemy database, select "Graphics," then "Enemy Model" from the main menu.

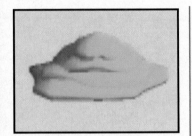

Enemy #0: Slime

Enemy #4: Beholder

Enemy #8: Cyclops

Enemy #12: Greater Demon

Enemy #1: Imp

Enemy #5: Werewolf

Enemy #9: Minotaur

Enemy #13: Arch Lord

Enemy #2: Goblin

Enemy #6: Ogre

Enemy #10: Centuar

Enemy #14: Protector

Enemy #3: Gargoyle

Enemy #7: Lizard Warrior

Enemy #11: Demon

Enemy #15: Warlock

Enemy #16: Titan

Enemy #17: Iron Giant

Enemy #18: Devourer

Enemy #19: Familiar

Enemy #20: Gremlin King

Enemy #21: Yeti

Enemy #22: Snow Beast

Enemy #23: Pegasus

Enemy #24: Wild Animal

Enemy #25: King Boar

Enemy #26: Dire Hound

Enemy #27: Chimera

Enemy #28: Griffon

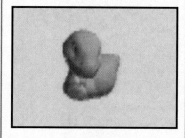

Enemy #29: Snake

Enemy #30: Hatchling

Enemy #31: Raptor

Enemy #32: Dragon

Enemy #33: Bone Dragon

Enemy #34: Wyvern

Enemy #35: Giant Bird

Enemy #36: Vampire Bat

Enemy #41: Frog Man

Enemy #46: Kraken

Enemy #51: Dragonfly

Enemy #37: Buzzard

Enemy #42: Crab

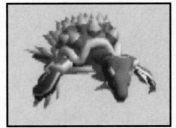

Enemy #47: Sea Dragon

Enemy #52: Crawler

Enemy #38: Bird Man

Enemy #43: Horned Fish

Enemy #48: Turtle Dragon

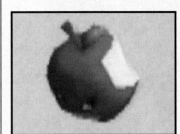

Enemy #53: Insectus

Enemy #39: Phoenix

Enemy #44: Seahorse

Enemy #49: Wasp Warrior

Enemy #54: Rotten Apple

Enemy #40: Starfish

Enemy #45: Merman

Enemy #50: Killer Bee

Enemy #55: Pumpkin Head

Enemy #56: Fungus

Enemy #61: Ghost

Enemy #66: Mummy

Enemy #71: Demon Egg

Enemy #57: Killer Flower

Enemy #62: Cherub

Enemy #67: Undead Warrior

Enemy #72: Gremlin Vase

Enemy #58: Man-eater

Enemy #63: Demon Skull

Enemy #68: Arch Demon

Enemy #73: Gremlin Chest

Enemy #59: Treant

Enemy #64: Genie

Enemy #69: Arch Angel

Enemy #74: Living Sword

Enemy #60: Spirits

Enemy #65: Zombie

Enemy #70: Bomber

Enemy #75: Living Armor

Enemy #76: Spade Soldier

Enemy #77: Diamond Soldier

Enemy #78: Club Soldier

Enemy #79: Heart Soldier

Enemy #80: Sentinel

Enemy #81: Golem

Enemy #82: Pharaoh

Enemy #83: Elder

Enemy #84: Timekeeper

Enemy #85: Gatekeeper

Enemy #86: Warrior

Enemy #87: Assassin

Enemy #88: Dragon Knight

Enemy #89: Pirate

Enemy #90: Joker

Enemy #91: Dragon

Enemy #92: Evoker

Enemy #93: Arch Mage

Enemy #94: Dwarf

Enemy #95: Amazon Warrior

Enemy #96: Witch

Enemy #98: Mystic

Enemy #100: Pugilist

Enemy #102: Overlord

Enemy #97: Hunter

Enemy #99: Alien

Enemy #101: Fighter

Enemy #103: Warlord

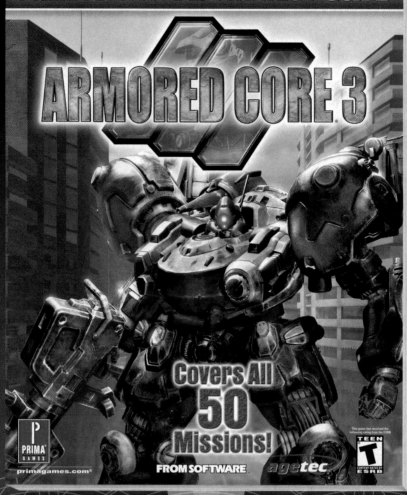